Reinventing the University

Managing and Financing Institutions
of Higher Education
1998

NONPROFIT LAW, FINANCE, AND MANAGEMENT SERIES

The Art of Planned Giving: Understanding Donors and the Culture of Giving by Douglas E. White

Beyond Fund Raising: New Strategies for Nonprofit Investment and Innovation by Kay Grace

Charity, Advocacy, and the Law by Bruce R. Hopkins

The Complete Guide to Nonprofit Management by Smith, Bucklin & Associates

Critical Issues in Fund Raising edited by Dwight Bulingame

Developing Affordable Housing: A Practical Guide for Nonprofit Organizations by Bennett L. Hecht

Financial and Accounting Guide for Not-for-Profit Organizations, Fifth Edition by Malvern J. Gross, Jr., Richard F. Larkin, Roger S. Bruttomesso, John J. McNally, Price Waterhouse LLP

Financial Management for Nonprofit Organizations by Jo Ann Hankin, Alan Seidner, and John Zietlow

Financial Planning for Nonprofit Organizations by Jody Blazek

Fund-Raising: Evaluating and Managing the Fund Development Process by James M. Greenfield

Fund-Raising Fundamentals: A Guide to Annual Giving for Professionals and Volunteers by James M. Greenfield

Fund-Raising Regulation: A State-by-State Handbook of Registration Forms, Requirements, and Procedures by Seth Perlman and Betsy Hills Bush

Grantseeker's Toolkit: A Comprehensive Guide to Finding Funding by Cheryl S. New and James Quick

Intermediate Sanctions: Curbing Nonprofit Abuse by Bruce R. Hopkins and D. Benson Tesdahl

International Guide to Nonprofit Law by Lester A. Salamon and Stefan Toepler & Associates

The Law of Fund-Raising, Second Edition by Bruce R. Hopkins

The Law of Tax-Exempt Healthcare Organizations by Thomas K. Hyatt and Bruce R. Hopkins

The Law of Tax-Exempt Organizations, Sixth Edition by Bruce R. Hopkins

The Legal Answer Book for Nonprofit Organizations by Bruce R. Hopkins

A Legal Guide to Starting and Managing a Nonprofit Organization, Second Edition by Bruce R. Hopkins

Managing Affordable Housing: A Practical Guide to Creating Stable Communities by Bennett L. Hecht, Local Initiatives Support Corporation, and James Stockard

Nonprofit Boards: Roles, Responsibilities, and Performance by Diane J. Duca

Nonprofit Compensation and Benefits Practices by Applied Research and Development Institute International, Inc.

The Nonprofit Counsel by Bruce R. Hopkins

The Nonprofit Guide to the Internet by Robbin Zeff

Nonprofit Investment Policies: A Practical Guide to Creation and Implementation by Robert Fry, Jr.

The Nonprofit Law Dictionary by Bruce R. Hopkins

Nonprofit Employment Law: Compensation, Benefits, and Regulation by David G. Samuels and Howard Pianko

Nonprofit Litigation: A Practical Guide with Forms and Checklists by Steve Bachmann

The Nonprofit Handbook, Second Edition: Volume I—Management by Tracy Daniel Connors

The Nonprofit Handbook, Second Edition: Volume II—Fund Raising by Jim Greenfield

The Nonprofit Manager's Resource Dictionary by Ronald A. Landskroner

Nonprofit Organizations' Business Forms: Disk Edition by John Wiley & Sons, Inc.

Partnerships and Joint Ventures Involving Tax-Exempt Organizations by Michael I. Sanders

Planned Giving: Management, Marketing, and Law by Ronald R. Jordan and Katelyn L. Quynn

Private Foundations: Tax Law and Compliance by Bruce R. Hopkins and Jody Blazek

Program Related Investments: A Technical Manual for Foundations by Christie I Baxter

Reengineering Your Nonprofit Organization: A Guide to Strategic Transformation by Alceste T. Pappas

Reinventing the University: Managing and Financing Institutions of Higher Education by Sandra L. Johnson and Sean C. Rush, Coopers & Lybrand, L.L.P.

Strategic Communications for Nonprofit Organizations: Seven Steps to Creating a Successful Plan by Janel Radtke

Strategic Planning for Nonprofit Organizations: A Practical Guide and Workbook by Michael Allison and Jude Kaye, Support Center for Nonprofit Management

Streetsmart Financial Basics for Nonprofit Managers by Thomas A. McLaughlin

A Streetsmart Guide to Nonprofit Mergers and Networks by Thomas A. McLaughlin

Successful Marketing Strategies for Nonprofit Organizations by Barry J. McLeish

The Tax Law of Charitable Giving by Bruce R. Hopkins

The Tax Law of Colleges and Universities by Bertrand M. Harding

Tax Planning and Compliance for Tax-Exempt Organizations: Forms, Checklists, Procedures, Second Edition by Jody Blazek

The Universal Benefits of Volunteering: A Practical Workbook for Nonprofit Organizations, Volunteers and Corporations by Walter P. Pidgeon, Jr.

The Volunteer Management Handbook by Tracy Daniel Connors

Reinventing the University

Managing and Financing Institutions
of Higher Education
1998

Edited by
Clark L. Bernard
Sandra L. Johnson
Jillinda J. Kidwell
PricewaterhouseCoopers

John Wiley & Sons, Inc.
New York • Chichester • Weinheim • Brisbane • Singapore • Toronto

This book is printed on acid-free paper. ∞

Copyright © 1998 by PricewaterhouseCoopers. All rights reserved.
Published by John Wiley & Sons, Inc.

Published simultaneously in Canada.

This publication is designed to provide accurate and authoritative information in regard
to the subject matter covered. It is sold with the understanding that the publisher is not
engaged in rendering professional services. If professional advice or other expert
assistance is required, the services of a competent professional person should be sought.

Library of Congress Cataloging in Publication Data:
Reinventing the university : managing and financing institutions of
   higher education / [edited and compiled by] Sandra L. Johnson, Sean C.
   Rush.
      p.   cm.—(Nonprofit law, finance, and management series)
   Includes bibliographical refeences and index.
   ISBN 0-471-10452-3 (cloth : acid-free paper)
   ISBN 0-471-19596-0 (paper)
   1. Universities and colleges—United States—Administration.
2. Universities and colleges—United States—Finance.   I. Johnson,
Sandra L.   II. Rush, Sean C.   III. Series.
LB2341.R42   1995
378.73—dc20   94-45421

Printed in the United States of America
10 9 8 7 6 5 4 3 2 1

SUBSCRIPTION NOTICE

This Wiley product is updated on a periodic basis with supplements to reflect important changes in the subject matter. If you purchased this product directly from John Wiley & Sons, Inc., we have recently recorded your subscription for this update service.

If, however, you purchased tihs product from a bookstore and wish to receive (1) the current update at no additional charge, and (2) future updates and revised or related volumes billed separately with a 30-day examination review, please send your name, company name (if applicable), address, and the title of the product to:

Supplement Department
John Wiley & Sons, Inc.
One Wiley Drive
Somerset, NJ 08875
1-800-225-5945

For customers outside the United States, please contact the Wiley office nearest you:

Professional & Reference Division
John Wiley & Sons Canada, Ltd.
22 Worcester Road
Rexdale, Ontario M9W 1L1
CANADA
(416) 675-3580
1-800-567-4797
FAX (416) 675-6599

John Wiley & Sons, Ltd.
Baffins Lane
Chichester
West Sussex, PO19 1UD
UNITED KINGDOM
(44) (243)779777

Jacaranda Wiley Ltd.
PRT Division
PO Box 174
North Ryde, NSW 2113
AUSTRALIA
(02) 805-1100
FAX (02) 805-1597

John Wiley & Sons (SEA) Pte. Ltd.
37 Jalan Pemimpin
Block B # 05-04
Union Industrial Building
SINGAPORE 2057
(65) 258-1157

ABOUT THE EDITORS

Clark L. Bernard, MBA, CPA, serves as the co-chairman of Pricewater-houseCoopers's National Higher Education and Not-for-Profit Industry Group. This group coordinates the firm's services to colleges and universities and keeps its higher education professionals and clients informed about industry developments in management, finance, taxation, legislation, accounting and reporting. Mr. Bernard has extensive experience working with leading colleges and universities as a business assurance (audit) partner. He has served as the senior client services partner on some of Coopers & Lybrand's most visible and complex public and private universities, research institutions, and academic medical centers.

Recognizing the challenging environment in which higher education operates, he works with senior university management, trustees, and leading higher education associations on emerging management, governance, accounting, and business issues. He also consults with regulatory and stanard-setting bodies about initiatives that directly affect higher education and not-for-profit organizations.

Mr. Bernard serves as the firm's spokesman on matters relating to the higher education and not-for-profit sectors. He is a frequent speaker at industry conferences. He is a member of the National Association of College and University Business Officers (NACUBO).

Sandra L. Johnson, MBA, CPA, is a director in PricewaterhouseCoopers's National Higher Education and Not-for-Profit Industry Group.

Ms. Johnson's publication include *Understanding College and University Financial Statements, Financial Reporting and Contributions: A Decision Making Guide to FASB Nos. 116 & 117*, in collaboration with other authors from Coopers & Lybrand and Robert Turner from Babson College, and *The Audit Committee: A Key to Financial Accountability in Nonprofit Organizations*. She also has written a chapter in *Measuring Institutional Performance in Higher Education* with Joel Myerson from Coopers & Lybrand. With Sean C. Rush, Ms. Johnson co-authored *The Decaying American Campus*. She also wrote the annual *Agenda Priorities* column in the Association of Governing Boards of Universities and Colleges publication, (AGB) *Trusteeship*, and articles for the NACUBO *Business Officer* and is the editor of Coopers & Lybrand's quarterly *Insights: A Journal for Colleges, Universities, and Other Not-for-Profit Organizations*.

She is a member of NACUBO and the Eastern Association of College and University Business Officers.

Jillinda Jonker Kidwell, MBA, is the partner-in-charge of PricewaterhouseCoopers Higher Education Consulting Practice which provides consulting support to help colleges and universities plan for and implement change. Her consulting experience is devoted to helping large, complex research universities and their academic medical centers respond to external challenges through planning, strategic repositioning, restructuring and reengineering. Recognizing the important role of change in management, she works with senior leadership to develop the infrastructure required to realize the results envisioned by reengineering.

She has published extensively on process redesign. In 1994 she coauthored two NACUBO monographs entitled, "Business Process Redesign in Higher Education" and "Performance Measurement Systems in Higher Education," and wrote a chapter on managing transformation in higher education for the John Wiley & Sons, Inc., book, *Reinventing the University: Managing and Financing Institutions of Higher Education.* This article has been reprinted as part of NACUBO's *Executive Strategy Series* and included in a recent publication entitled *The Paradigm Shift.*

Ms. Kidwell is a frequent speaker and lecturer in the subject of transforming higher education including NACUBO Professional Development Workshops, firm-sponsored Executive Issues in Higher Education Seminars, and NACUBO regional meetings. In addition, she has presented seminars on managing organizational change to various management groups ranging from local non-profit organizations to university senior management teams and to business executives in eastern Europe.

ABOUT THE CONTRIBUTORS

Molly Corbett Broad currently serves as President of the University of North Carolina, which comprises 16 campuses enrolling over 154,000 students. Prior to joining UNC in July 1997, she helped to lead the California State University for 5 years, beginning in 1992 as senior vice chancellor for administration and finance and assuming the position of executive vice chancellor and chief operating officer of the 23-campus system one year later. She is one of the three founding board members of Internet 2 and also serves on the boards of the International Council for Distance Education and the International Business Education Roundtable. She also sits on the advisory boards of the Mellon Foundation, the National Technology Task Force, and the National Association of State Universities and Land-Grant Colleges. She has written and spoken widely on the topics of strategic planning for higher education and emerging technologies.

Thomas R. Donnelly, Jr. is Senior Vice President of The Jefferson Group, a flourishing health care government relations practice in Washington, D.C. He has served as Assistant Secretary for Legislation and, later, Acting Secretary of the U.S. Department of Health and Human Services. Mr. Donnelly has been active in all major health care policy debates since the early 1980s and was the Administration's primary lobbyist during enactment of the Prospective Payment System for Medicare in 1983.

The Honorable Jerry MacArthur Hultin is currently serving since November 1997, as Under Secretary of the Navy, the Navy and Marine Corps' second highest civilian leader. Formerly, he was Vice Chairman of Jefferson Partners, L.L.C., an investment banking firm, and Chairman of Hultin & Associates, Inc., a management consulting firm.

Donald M. Norris is President of Strategic Initiatives, Inc., a management consulting firm in Herndon, Virginia, specializing in strategic thinking and organizational transformation. Dr. Norris is widely recognized as an author, including a three-volume series on transformation published by the Society for College and University Planning: *Transforming Higher Education: A Vision for Learning in the 21st Century*,

Unleashing the Power of Perpetual Learning, and *Revolutionary Strategy for the Knowledge Age.* He is currently working on a number of projects for corporations, universities, and associations involving the deployment of expeditionary strategy and products. A description of these activities and a complete list of publications may be found at www.strategicinitiatives.com.

Stuart H. Rakoff is Vice President of Jefferson Partners, L.L.C., an investment banking firm and works with a number of organizations including government agencies, national managed care companies, and information technology providers to formulate and execute strategic planning and organizational redesign. Dr. Rakoff previously was a senior executive with a national pension and health care trust and was Director of Manpower Planning for the Department of Defense. He earned his undergraduate degree at Colby College and his doctorate in Political Science at the University of Minnesota.

Donald Langenberg, Ph.D., an eminent physicist and nationally known advocate for higher education, has headed the 13-member University Systems of Maryland since 1990. Dr. Langenberg's leadership has shaped USM throughout its formative years—a decade of change in American higher education marked by new fiscal constraints, rapidly evolving technologies, and fundamental shifts in the demographics of the nation's college-going population.

Don Peppers, is a Partner of Marketing 1 to 1/Peppers and Rogers Group. He is also a coauthor (with Martha Rogers, Ph.D.) of the ground breaking international best-seller *The One To One Future: Building Relationships One Customer at a Time* and *Enterprise One to One: Tools for Competing in the Interactive Age,* awarded a top-rated five stars by *The Wall Street Journal.* Don Peppers and Martha Rogers were named 1998 Direct Marketers of the Year by Direct Marketing Days in New York.

Martha Rogers, Ph.D., is a Partner of Marketing 1 to 1/Peppers and Rogers Group. She is also a coauthor (with Don Peppers) of the ground breaking international best-seller *The One To One Future: Building Relationships One Customer at a Time* and *Enterprise One to One: Tools for Competing in the Interactive Age,* awarded a top-rated five stars by *The Wall Street Journal.* Don Peppers and Martha Rogers were named 1998 Direct Marketers of the Year by Direct Marketing Days in New York.

ABOUT THE CONTRIBUTORS

Grady Means, is the Managing Partner of Strategy Consulting at PricewaterhouseCoopers. He was formerly Special Assistant to the Vice President of the United States, and Assistant to the Secretary of Health Education and Welfare as well as a staff member of the Stanford Graduate School of Business.

Preface

THE TRANSFORMATION OF HIGHER EDUCATION IN THE DIGITAL AGE

Coopers & Lybrand L.L.P. hosted a roundtable discussion on the transformation of higher education in the digital age in July 1997 at the Aspen Institute in Maryland.[1] This volume presents some of the key messages from our discussions in Maryland. We are pleased that many of the speakers and facilitators from our roundtable also agreed to contribute chapters to this volume, our second supplement to *Reinventing the University: Managing and Financing Institutions of Higher Education.*

Trends Forcing Change in Higher Education

Colleges and universities need to prepare for major upheaval in the digital age. Broadly speaking, the trends include changes in market demand and the impact of technology on the industry. More specifically, we highlight five significant trends here.

The market for learning is increasing rapidly. According to demographic projections, baby boomers, those 40 to 59 years old, will be the fastest growing segment of the U.S. population between 1996 and 2005.[2] More of them than ever before are expected to seek additional education. The "echo boomers," those who are 10 to 19 years of age, are another rapidly growing population segment in the United States. Echo boomers are the next wave of students enrolling in college. A new reality for workers of all ages is that lifelong learning has become a necessity. After lagging for several years, the growing U.S. population (along

---

[1] Our roundtable was sponsored by Coopers & Lybrand's Learning Partnership, a program that began in 1994. It is designed to be an interactive exchange of dialogue on a given topic that provides interactive, continuous learning for everyone involved.

[2] U.S. Census data.

with the foreign students who seek entry) and the need for lifelong learning are dramatically increasing the size of the potential learning market.

Buyers are more demanding. Today's students are technologically sophisticated consumers who expect services that are as user-friendly, accessible, and convenient as automatic teller machines. Until recently, they have not significantly influenced the traditional delivery of services. The burgeoning market of lifelong learners is likely to demand services *and* education that are:

- Available at the time and place, and in the medium, of students' choosing
- Logically bundled and hassle-free
- One-stop or no-stop
- Cost-effective
- High-tech but personal
- Integrated, seamless, and collaborative
- Consistent and dependable

Technology is creating powerful substitutes for traditional products.[3] The technology of the future is likely to include instructional software. If it could truly capture the many facets of learning, such software could easily substitute for certain campus-based instruction (or at least be a substantial part of the delivery system). In fact, research indicates that the creation of a mere 25 courses would serve an estimated 80 percent of total undergraduate enrollment in core undergraduate courses. The software would serve an estimated 50 percent of the total student enrollment in community colleges, as well as an estimated 35 percent of the total student enrollment in four-year institutions. And as we already see in the professional continuing education sector of the learning industry, some organizations are already dependent on instructional software.

---

[3]This section is based on material presented by Dr. Carol A. Twigg, Vice President, Educom, a nonprofit consortium of more than 600 colleges and universities and 120 corporations dedicated to the transformation of higher education through the application of information technology, at the July 1997 Learning Partnership sponsored by Coopers & Lybrand L.L.P. at the Aspen Institute in Maryland. Dr. Twigg leads Educom's National Learning Infrastructure Initiative (NLII). For more information, you may want to visit its website at http://educom.edu/program/nlii/nliiHome.html.

Software that captures the many facets of the learning process and can substitute for campus-based instruction is not yet on the market. This is partially due to high costs. Developing high-quality instructional software might cost $3 million per course. The annual maintenance cost might run to $500,000, not counting marketing and distribution.

At a $3 million investment, a "core" course (e.g., biology 101, calculus 101, etc.) could be replaced with an absolutely terrific technology-based course. The technology-based course could be supplemented with a 24-hour international help desk, offering 8 hours of help in the United States, 8 hours in Europe, etc. At this scale, it would be conceivable to spend $3 million on a course and develop a truly effective learning tool, one that would transform education delivery methods.

Competition from nontraditional competitors is increasing. The specter of Microsoft haunts many industries, including higher education. Imagine, if you will, the following (completely fictitious) scenario. Suppose that the chairman of Microsoft contacts the governor of California and proposes to serve more students and achieve higher performance standards at two-thirds the amount currently paid to the California State University System. How do you suppose the governor might react to this proposal?

More immediate challenges for the higher education industry are new entrants like the University of Phoenix, Sylvan Learning Systems, and corporate universities. The University of Phoenix, for instance, currently enrolls more than 40,000 students across geographical boundaries and is serving an important niche market of adult learners (the average undergraduate at Phoenix is 34 years old and has been working for 13 years).[4] Also, corporate training programs are increasing at a record pace—from a handful in the 1980s to 400 in 1994 to more than 1,000 in 1997.[5] In fact, a graduate degree can be obtained from Arthur D. Little's School of Management.[6]

Barriers to entry are coming down, making market entry relatively easy. Changing the federal student financial aid policy would alter the competitive landscape dramatically. In fact, provisions presented to the Department of Education by institutions and other constituents for inclusion in the Higher Education Amendments (HEA) proposal to

[4]*The Chronicle of Higher Education*, June 6, 1997, 32–33.

[5]Thomas E. Moore, "The Corporate University: Transforming Management Education," *Accounting Horizons*, March 1997, 78.

[6]*Id.* at 77.

Congress include lifting restrictions on certain distance learning programs so that they may be eligible for Title IV funds. (The HEA as amended is the governing legislation for the major federal student financial aid programs supporting higher education, including such Title IV programs as Stafford Loans, Perkins Loans, Direct Loans, and others.) Such a move by the Department of Education would change the rules of the game, give new entrants sources of funding, and increase buying power for nontraditional students.

In addition, technology removes two other significant barriers to entry. The first is the need for bricks and mortar. Distributed learning provides educational opportunities in any place; traditional campuses are not necessary. The second involves full-time faculty. Distributed learning enables a small number of professors to reach a huge market of students.

On the Brink of Structural Change

The impact caused by the convergence of these trends—the exploding market for learning, new learning technologies, and the lowering of barriers to entry—in the higher education industry is potentially substantial. Taken together, they are capable of creating an inflection point, thereby dramatically altering the structure of the higher education industry. In manufacturing, health care, advertising, and the airline industries, for example, competitive forces shifted so dramatically that they caused massive, industry-wide restructuring.

There are visible signs that competitive forces may soon cause massive structural changes in the higher education industry. Those familiar with Michael Porter's views in his book *Competitive Strategy* understand that industry-wide restructuring is imminent when the five industry forces[7] are in flux. A cursory analysis using Porter's competitive forces framework suggests that this condition exists in higher education. The very structure of higher education is poised for change. As has occurred in other industries, it is likely that there will be mergers, consolidations, and shakeouts.

An analysis of the transformation of the health care industry, and its similarities to higher education, strengthens the argument that structural change is on the horizon. Thomas Donnelly, Jerry Hultin, and Stuart Rakoff discuss this in Chapter 3, "The Revolution in Health Care and a Prognosis for Higher Education." They examine the role of physicians several years ago and now, and question whether the role of faculty might shift in a similar fashion.

---

[7]Porter's five forces are the entry of new competitors, threat of substitutes, bargaining power of buyers, bargaining power of suppliers, and rivalry among existing competitors.

Health care was a growth industry subsidized by federal dollars and characterized by physicians making the major decisions in health care delivery. In the 1970s and 1980s, faint cries for change were heard. At first, change occurred slowly and incrementally. By the 1990s, however, a major revolution had occurred in health care. Today, the health care industry has consolidated and drastically reduced its costs. Large purchasers, some for-profit, drive the marketplace and set performance standards. Physicians now answer to the HMOs, and both must meet the demands of the payer groups: government, employers, and insurance organizations.

The first wave of "winners" in the health care industry have been the largest, lowest-cost providers.[8] Can this scenario be repeated in higher education? Although the cycle of adaptation in higher education seems to roughly mirror that of the health care industry, it also lags it by about 10 years. Nevertheless, large, low-cost educational providers are emerging. Institutions of all sizes have begun cost-reduction initiatives on the administrative front, and some have followed on the academic side of the enterprise. Investments in technology are being made, both to drive down costs and to improve the quality of service for students and others. Consolidation is already under way, notably in academic medical centers. It remains to be seen whether the transformation of higher education will continue to mirror that of health care or whether it will take a new turn.

Recommendations

Clearly, the competitive landscape in higher education is rapidly changing, and the industry may be on the brink of major structural change. This environment requires rapid responses. Those institutions that do not envision the future and their unique role in it do so at their own peril. This is not a "do-nothing" situation. Every institution has the potential to gain or lose; for some, dramatic action will be required just to stay in place. Absent simple answers, what can be done? We suggest that institutions start by considering the following recommendations.

Ask strategic questions to involve key constituents and begin thinking through solutions that are appropriate for your institution. Start with those in the

---

[8]It may be important for higher education to note that some experts suggest that the next phase of change in health care—and the next wave of winners—are likely to be *low-cost* providers that also provide the *highest quality* of patient care. Information technology, used thus far to drive down costs, will be used to enhance the quality of care and increase patient satisfaction. Once cost efficiency is achieved, the next competitive edge is likely to be *quality*.

chart at the end of this preface and add others. Along with carefully considered answers, they can help shape the parameters of a solution.

Consider new approaches to strategy development.   The process of strategy development readies leaders to engineer the strategic structure of their institution to take full advantage of advances in technology and to pursue emerging new market opportunities rapidly. What is strategy? According to Jill Kidwell and Grady Means in Chapter 5, "Strategies for the Future," *strategy* is what a university does to sustain and grow its value into the future—and the key word is "does."

The authors note that higher education's traditional strategic planning processes no longer apply. Rather, institutions need transformational strategy to cope with fundamental shifts in the higher education industry. "Doing" transformational strategy requires:

- Preparing up front but with the end in mind

- Using a solid analytical framework to identify transformational strategies

- Determining and categorizing potential strategies

- Using a visionary conference to develop a compelling vision and to narrow the set of strategic alternatives

- Committing to a handful of strategies

Undertake expeditionary initiatives to test hypotheses and develop core competencies.   Institutions and those who lead them must be nimble, with all that this word implies—including being willing to ask questions that do not have ready answers and experimenting without knowing exactly where the experiments will lead. Institutions may strike out in several directions and take paths that cannot be envisioned from the outset. In the process, competencies will be learned that could not have been learned without embarking on such expeditions. Donald Norris (President, Strategic Initiatives) and Donald Langenberg (President, University of Maryland) recommend the following six competencies in Chapter 1, "Expeditionary Strategy and Products for the Knowledge Age:"

- Strong leadership

- Know-how about managing rapid change

- Information technology skills

- New types of products, services, and interactivity

- New financial paradigms

- Ability to manage strategic alliances (like those noted later)

Form partnerships and alliances. According to Molly Corbett Broad, President of the University of North Carolina, who contributed Chapter 3, "Strategic Partnerships: What Universities and Corporations Can Do Together," partnerships will be critical components of future strategies. They are likely to fall into two categories, institutional and corporate.

- *Institutional alliances.* Rather than being part of the Western Governors University, the public and private universities in California have formed their own virtual university. The California Virtual University will build on existing distributed learning activities, increase access, provide a full array of educational certification, and rely on intra- and intercampus infrastructure.

- *Corporate alliances.* The California State University System (CSU) is partnering with Warner Brothers, certain high schools in California and Alabama, and national and regional telecommunications companies to train digital animation artists for the entertainment industry. The CSU also is partnering with Simon & Schuster, the publishing giant, to offer teacher training programs. Simon & Schuster has provided front-end funds and the CSU-based authors of textbooks on teacher education will deliver five courses basic to the curriculum not only on CSU campuses but also in key locations throughout the state.

Adopt mass customization strategies. Customers are becoming more savvy and more demanding. As a result, mass customization strategies, such as personalized marketing through technology to a large customer base, are becoming increasingly applicable to higher education. Mass customization techniques save money *and* increase customer loyalty, according to Don Peppers and Dr. Martha Rogers, the founding partners of Marketing 1:1 and the authors of Chapter 2, "The Business End of the One-to-One Future in Learning and Credentialing."

Mass customization requires up-front investment in technology to track the necessary data for each customer and to identify the most worthwhile customers. Once the investment is made, the ability to lock in particular customers (including, in higher education's case, students, grantors, donors, and other constituents) and provide them with superior service provides competitive advantage.

Levi Strauss is creating competitive advantage by offering customized blue jeans. The customer is measured first and then places an order for blue jeans. Working with thousands of premanufactured components, Levi Strauss assembles about 10,000 very personal combinations. The customer pays a premium of almost $20 for these custom-fit jeans, although they actually cost less to produce than other jeans because there are no inventory costs. And it is well worth the extra cost to the customer, because the jeans fit perfectly every time.

What if an institution employed mass customization techniques in its academic program? Say it studied student learning styles, for example, and found that they could be grouped into a few categories: those who learn most efficiently in groups; those who learn most efficiently by using hands-on techniques, and so on. What if this institution then tailored its academic programs to these 10 different learning styles? Could a program that was guaranteed to be effective command a premium price?

In Summary

It was clear to those assembled at Coopers & Lybrand's Learning Partnership on the transformation of higher education in the digital age that great forces for change are at work. What was less clear was the timing of major structural changes and the investments these changes portend. In five years, will the influencers and leaders of American higher education recognize the industry they now serve? How about in 10 years?

At one extreme, higher education is ripe for "FedExing," much like the U.S. Postal Service was. Under this scenario, new entrants unencumbered by physical plant, tenure costs, and an industry mindset could rewrite the rules, capturing the most lucrative segments and leaving non-branded institutions to serve the less profitable markets. However, some assert that there will always be a demand for face-to-face learning environments. They point out that the basic higher education model has not changed fundamentally for over 700 years.

Can our colleges and universities afford to wait and see what the future will bring for them? We think not. Like the contributing authors to this volume, we believe that the digital age is already transforming higher education, and will continue to do so. Above all, it is key for higher education to keep orienting itself toward the future and whatever it may hold.

KEY QUESTIONS THAT UNIVERSITY EXECUTIVES SHOULD BE ASKING

... About the Market and Strategy

- Have we considered "doing" transformational strategy?
- How has our competition changed over the past five years?
- Who are our current and potential competitors and how should we respond to them?
- How might our relationship with our suppliers (K–12 schools and vendors, for example) change in the digital age?
- How might our relationship with our buyers (states, parents, employers, for example) change in the digital age?
- Are we seeking corporate partners or other types of alliances for any new initiatives?
- Have we assessed—and found favorable—our position in the marketplace and the demand for our courses and programs?
- Have we defined institutional priorities? Are we allocating resources in accordance with them?
- Are there sufficient financial resources and personnel to implement our plans?
- Do we have a distributed learning strategy?

... About Technology

- Do we have the organization, services, and infrastructure needed to support the development and design of technology-based course materials?
- Is our network infrastructure reliable and does it have the interoperability we need?
- Are our technology initiatives connected to our institutional strategies and mission?
- Are we making sufficient progress in information technologies to keep our institution competitively positioned to attract students, faculty, and staff?
- Is technology sufficiently available in our classrooms, libraries, computer labs, and departments?

... About Human Resources

- Do our HR programs support our institutional strategy?
- Are our employees working productively? Are they maximizing the anticipated changes and improvements from our technology projects?
- Do we know what skills and competencies are required in our changing environment and have we ensured that our employees have those skills and competencies?
- Do we have a pay and reward philosophy? Do we have a performance management approach that is linked with the university's goals?

(continued)

KEY QUESTIONS THAT UNIVERSITY EXECUTIVES SHOULD BE ASKING
(Continued)

- Do we have an effective performance evaluation system for tenured faculty? For staff?
- Is our recruitment and retention strategy for staff effective? Is our recruitment and retention strategy for faculty working?
- Could our HR organization serve the institution more effectively?
- Does the structure of our organization maximize service and organizational effectiveness?

. . . About Student Services
- Are we meeting and exceeding the expectations of our students related to service quality, timeliness, responsiveness, and access?
- Are we using mass customization strategies to our best advantage?
- Do we have a student/learner-centered service organization with cross-trained staff capable of handling students' issues and questions in one stop?
- Are our faculty advisors and staff using their personal interactions with students to provide insight and advice instead of to resolve transaction-related issues?
- Are resources allocated to the activities that are most highly valued by our students and that most contribute to their retention and overall satisfaction?
- Have we defined a measure of value and are we measuring the value our student services organization provides?
- Do we have a single integrated student services database?

. . . About Research Administration
- Has increased competition for research funding affected our research programs?
- Is our research administration process working well?
- Has research funding from industry increased and are we forming industry partnerships?
- Do faculty complain that they do not know where or how to find access to funding opportunities, especially from nongovernmental sources?
- Are we organized so that we can deal effectively with corporate sponsors?
- Will we be ready for the demands of federal agencies to interact electronically?

Contents

CONTENTS

The Expeditionary Framework

Chapter One
Expeditionary Strategy and Products for the Knowledge Age

Expeditionary Strategy and Products for the Knowledge Age

DONALD N. LANGENBERG
University of Maryland

DONALD M. NORRIS
Strategic Initiatives, Inc.

1.1 INTRODUCTION

A new variety of strategy and product development will be needed to
create learning products and experiences that meet the emerging standards of the Knowledge Age learner. "Expeditionary" is the adjective
that best describes this new approach. Expeditionary strategy and product development have been the norm in the software and laptop computer industries. They are about to become the norm in the learning
industry, as our next generation of learning products and experiences—
learningware, if you will—will have more in common with the patterns
and cadences of software development than with traditional curriculum development.

The first generation of an expeditionary approach is discernible in
today's leading-edge learning products. This chapter provides a vision
for the new breed of expeditionary strategy and products, then grounds
that vision in cases and examples.

The Knowledge Age will truly be the "Age of Learning." Learning
will be the primary source of sustainable competitive advantage for individuals, organizations, communities, and nations. Although learning
resources will flow freely across community, organizational, and national boundaries, infrastructure, cultural, social, and political characteristics will still differentiate among communities, organizations, and
nations. Successful communities with good leadership and infrastruc-
ture/culture will be recognized as "smart communities." In this environment, learning will be a growth industry.

1.1 INTRODUCTION

Technology Enables the Fusion of Activity

Technology enables us to perform activities not just better, but in fundamentally different ways. An apt metaphor for the impact of technology is integration—or even better, fusion. Technology will enable us to eliminate barriers of time, place, and sequence, fusing activities in ways that have been unfathomable until now. Looking back from the future, we will regard this fusion of activity as one of the signal accomplishments of the Knowledge Age.

In the Knowledge Age, learning will be fused with work, recreation, personal development, "edutainment," and even the expression of spirituality. Knowledge Age citizens will learn every day through long and productive lives. They will learn anywhere, anytime, just-in-time, and over and over again. Knowledge Age learners will use physical learning places and resources as gateways to virtual resources. These physical learning places will be everywhere: desktops and laptops, classrooms and boardrooms, academic malls and union halls, community learning centers, and homes of mentors.

New Standards for Learning Products and Experiences

The terms *continuing* and *lifelong* are inadequate to describe this species of learning that will be an integral aspect of life in the Knowledge Age. Four key adjectives emerge:

- Perpetual—Knowledge Age learning will be fused with work and other activities and will occur all the time and over and over again.

- Distributed—learners in every physical space will be linked with a pervasive atmosphere of virtual (on-line) learning resources.

- Interactive—interactivity will replace unidirectional educational delivery as the metaphor for learning.

- Collaborative—learners will function as members of learning teams and communities, not just as individuals.

Learning enterprises that successfully address the need for perpetual, distributed, interactive, collaborative learning will experience substantial growth in the 21st century, in spite of fierce competition. Those that do not will miss opportunities for growth. They may also lose their market share of existing learners to new competitors and new learning alternatives. Or they may see their revenues drop dramatically as new modes of learning revolutionize the value and price propositions for learning.

To be successful in the Knowledge Age, colleges and universities must be capable of creating learning products, services, and experiences that meet Knowledge Age standards of timeliness, responsiveness, customization, coherence, and cohesion. Learners get these standards of performance from other products and will expect these standards in their learning experiences.

1.2   LEARNING WILL BE A GROWTH INDUSTRY IN THE KNOWLEDGE AGE

Learning will be a growth industry in the Knowledge Age. This growth will be enabled by the emergence of a diverse range of learning experiences. Distinctive combinations of this diversity of learning will occur in all learning enterprises. These will include:

- Traditional courses and degrees, on-campus

- Traditional courses and degrees, on-campus distributed learning

- Distributed learning, off-campus

- Transformed learning, interactivity, and certification of mastery

The growth opportunities for these types of learning vary, as summarized in Exhibit 1–1.

Traditional Courses and Degrees, On-Campus

Traditional learning settings will not disappear. Neither will they escape change. Many institutions will deploy technology in ways that merely enhance the efficiency and/or effectiveness of existing courses and degrees. Other colleges and universities will use technology-supported learning tools to create distributed learning environments that blend physical and virtual learning, on-campus.

Traditional Courses and Degrees, On-Campus Distributed Learning

Distributed learning tools will enable traditional colleges and universities to enrich the experience of their on-campus learners and reach out to serve students beyond the physical domain of their own campuses. This will open substantial growth opportunities.

1.2 LEARNING WILL BE A GROWTH INDUSTRY

Exhibit 1–1
KNOWLEDGE AGE LEARNING WILL BE A GROWTH INDUSTRY

Types of Learning	Overall Growth Potential	Areas of Growth
• Traditional courses and degrees, on-campus	• Mature industry, limited growth	• Regions and nations where numbers of 17- to 24-year-olds are growing • Major opportunities in selected states and developing nations
• Virtual and distributed learning, off-campus	• Substantial growth	• Virtual learning as a component of distributed learning, all settings
• Transformed learning, interactivity, and certification of mastery	• Massive growth in perpetual, distributed, interactive learning	• Workplace and application-driven learning are the new frontier

On-campus learning is a mature industry with limited growth overall. Traditional courses and degrees, offered primarily on-campus, constitute a mature industry, with limited growth overall. Significant growth can occur in demographically booming states such as Texas, Arizona, Florida, and California. Demographically driven and economic development-driven growth in developing countries will bring substantial opportunities for providing virtual learning resources from institutions in developed countries. Institutions that fail to participate will miss real opportunities to hone competencies that could be used in their local markets.

Distributed learning will create dramatic changes on campus. Traditional campuses will be able to enrich the learning experience, shorten it for many students, and reduce costs for their on-campus students. They will also be able to accommodate larger traditional student populations without having to build new campuses. Distributed learning tools will lead to further transformation of learning.

New, flexible providers will grow their market share. Even in a mature market, enterprises that redefine the prevailing assumptions and practices of the industry can experience mercurial growth. This is already happening, as for-profit learning enterprises like the Apollo Group (University of Phoenix), DeVry, and Sylvan Learning Systems are increasing their market shares by providing distributed learning variations on traditional courses and degrees with greater standards of flexibility, convenience, customization, and coherence. This trend will accelerate.

Distributed Learning, Off-Campus

Colleges and universities are reaching off-campus through distance learning, extended learning, and virtual variations on traditional college and university offerings (virtual community colleges and virtual universities). These efforts are instrumental in extending higher learning to underserved populations, including global learning markets. Virtualized learning resources created through these efforts become the building blocks for creating distributed learning environments and for progressively transforming learning, interactivity, and certification of mastery.

Virtual learning resources will be a substantial growth area. The provision of virtual learning resources will drive distributed learning in the full panoply of learning settings. Using these tools, virtual universities, open universities, extended learning units of major universities, and other learning enterprises will participate in the explosive expansion of learning in flourishing international markets. They will then use the competencies developed in those settings to compete more effectively in developed markets.

Virtualize existing models, then revolutionize. The first step in applying Knowledge Age tools is to digitize our existing models. This is true not just in the learning industry, but also in other industries that are confronting the emergence of radically different Knowledge Age marketplaces. As we acquire insight through digitizing and realigning our virtual learning resources, truly transformed approaches will emerge to the production and staging of learning experiences and the measurement of attainment and certification of mastery.

The Western Governor's University (WGU) and other emerging virtual universities are excellent cases in point. The number of learners who will be interested in a fully virtual degree program will be relatively limited in the face of other, distributed options. But the tools and protocols being developed by WGU and its strategic allies—virtual learning tools, competency-based learning, skills banks for individuals, and the integration of virtual learning resources into existing institutions—will be used extensively by many individuals and institutions. It is difficult to predict which of their capabilities and services will be their major revenue generators five years from now.

Transformed Learning, Interactivity, Certification of Mastery, and Research

In developing virtual variations on traditional models, we will discover how to transform learning experiences. Interactivity-based learning, competency-based learning, mass customized learning, and separation of certification of mastery from teaching will emerge. The cottage-based industry approach to course development will be replaced by a team-based approach that creates scaleable products and adaptable new learning support products. The application of these new learning tools to workplace-centered learning and communities of reflective practitioners will lead to new levels of professional certification and mastery development.

Massive growth in perpetual, distributed, interactive learning. The greatest growth potential lies in transformed learning experiences that create perpetual, distributed, collaborative, and interactive opportunities for learning and certification of mastery. These opportunities will be most valuable to persons 22 years old and older, but they will profoundly change our approach to learning at all stages of life. Preparing learners with the skills and expectations for a life of perpetual learning will be a basic responsibility of all colleges and universities.

To be sure, the "educated person" has always practiced some kind of perpetual learning. But only 10 percent of the workers in most organizations practice "active learning." Perpetual, distributed, interactive learning will be fused into almost everyone's activities in the Knowledge Age. The percentage of active learners will be much greater. Distributed, perpetual learning will not be limited to a small class of the cognoscenti.

Virtual variations and transformed learning experiences will chip away at traditional, on-campus learning. Clearly, the availability of virtual learning resources will accelerate the development of distributed learning on campus. Many semi-traditional and nontraditional learners will find distributed or virtual offerings to be attractive alternatives to existing learning. As more profoundly transformed learning experiences emerge, they will be even more attractive as substitutes for traditional offerings, especially at the postbaccalaureate level.

The time frames for new learning will vary. Eventually, transformed learning will be the great growth segment of the learning industry, but these opportunities will require time to develop. Virtual variations on traditional learning and transformed learning will take time to gestate and reach critical mass. Exhibit 1–2 portrays probable time frames for the development of new learning.

As a mature industry, traditional learning will reach a plateau—it will likely even decline in the face of other alternatives, both virtual and transformed. Knowledge Age learning in total, however, will grow dramatically. In *Transforming Higher Education*, Norris and Dolence estimated that 20 to 28 million new learners in the United States could be accommodated by virtual and transformed learning opportunities. The global marketplace could be 100 million or more. Even if reality proves to be only a fraction of this total, the opportunities are staggering.

A New Type of Strategy and Product for the New Age

In his *Fortune* article, "Killer Strategies That Make Shareholders Rich," Gary Hamel outlined the importance of strategy innovation during periods of fundamental change, calling on enterprises to "[u]nleash the power of strategy innovation—the ability to reinvent the basis of competition within the existing industries and to invent entirely new

Exhibit 1–2
POTENTIAL TIME FRAMES FOR GROWTH IN LEARNING

Types of Learning	0–3 Years	3–5 Years	5–10 Years	10–15 Years
Traditional Learning	• Demographically driven growth	• Demographically driven growth	• Virtual and/or transformed options cut into traditional learning	• Options dramatically impact traditional learning
Virtual Variations	• Gestating	• Substantial growth	• Substantial growth	• Transformed learning cuts into virtual variations
Transformed Learning	• Gestating	• Gestating	• Substantial growth	• Massive growth

industries. Strategy innovation will be the next fundamental competitive advantage for enterprises around the world. Only nonlinear strategies can create significant new wealth" (Hamel 1997).

Strategy innovation needs to recognize that during a period of fundamental realignment, some of the basic assumptions of the industry are changed:

- Analysis of existing industry conditions is not the real key to success. Where will the industry begin and end and how is it changing? Those are the essential strategic questions.

- Focusing on current competitors is misplaced. New competitors are the ones who will surprise you. Moreover, it will become difficult to distinguish competitors, collaborators, suppliers, and allies.

- It's not you against the world. You may own only a part of the value chain—your suppliers and strategic allies may own the rest.

Strategic innovation is a basic competency for the successful Knowledge Age organization, according to Gary Hamel. In this context, "[t]he goal is not to develop 'perfect' strategies, but to develop strategies that take us in the right direction, and then progressively refine them through rapid experimentation and adjustment" (Hamel 1997).

These same insights apply to product development. The new breed of product will be "expeditionary" in nature.

1.3   THINKING IN THE FUTURE TENSE

To create learning experiences for the Knowledge Age, we must look beyond extrapolating our current experiences. This requires what Jennifer James calls "thinking in the future tense," that is, envisioning how life and learning will be different in the future, then planning from the future backward. New principles for strategic thinking and guidance for reinventing the higher learning industry will emerge. Revolutionary vision can be ripped back to the present, thereby "making the blue sky meet the road." This process will provide the insights to overcome barriers and strategies to move forward into the future.

Looking Beyond the Misleading Edge

During periods of fundamental change, the future cannot be understood by simply extrapolating the present forward into the future. To move forward to the Knowledge Age, one must be able to look beyond the misleading edge. This is true for a variety of reasons, including the fact that the world of learning we are experiencing today represents a misleading preview of the world five years from now. At that time, technology will enable us to fuse activities in ways that are unfathomable by today's standards.

Principles for Strategic Thinking

Gary Hamel suggests 10 principles that guide the revolutionizing of strategy. These principles are essential to strategic thinking during a period of fundamental change.

1. *Strategic planning isn't strategic.* Most strategic planning is about incrementalism, not discovering new futures. It is ritualistic and reductionist, even mindlessly extrapolative, exploring from today forward rather than from the future backward. So-called strategic planning involves a small cadre of planners, thereby failing to unleash the organization's creative potential. Such groups typically fail to challenge the industry's conventions or explore fundamental change in its boundaries. How can organizations smash the shackles of nonstrategic strategic planning?

2. *Strategy making must be subversive.* Accept nothing as sacred or preordained. Questioning the assumptions, shibboleths, and folk wisdoms of the organization and its industry is fundamental to putting the *strategic* back into planning. But is the leadership of the typical organization capable of subverting existing orthodoxy?

3. *The bottleneck is at the top of the bottle.* The leadership pyramid in our organizations is an Industrial Age artifact. The peak of the pyramid is less diverse, less in touch with customers, and less attuned to the patterns and cadences of the Knowledge Age than any other part of the organization. And strategy is formulated at the top of the pyramid. Is this any way to run a revolution?

4. *Revolutionaries exist in every organization.* Every organization contains people with visions of the future and a sense of the stultifying impact of organizational orthodoxy. Strategy-crafting processes must discover ways of engaging and giving voice to these people. We must water where the grass is green and engage latent revolutionaries in the strategy process.

5. *Change is not the problem, engagement is.* Hamel exposes two false assumptions held by senior executives: (a) People are against change, and (b) only the heroic leader can drag a timid and backward-looking organization into the future. Too often, the codeword "change" is used by top leadership as an anesthetic to introduce a wrenching restructuring or reorganization. This is more about covering for past mistakes of leadership than opening up new opportunities. In reality, staff are ready to embrace change when it means opportunities for growth, exerting greater control over one's destiny, or stealing a march on complacent competitors.

6. *Strategy making must be more democratic.* The capacity to think creatively about strategy is distributed widely throughout an enterprise. In inclusive strategy-seeking exercises, some of the best ideas come from junior employees. The hierarchy of experience must be supplemented by the hierarchy of imagination in constituting strategy. This means including younger employees, participants from geographical peripheries, and newcomers.

7. *Anyone can be a strategy activist.* Senior managers must welcome front-line employees and middle managers to become strategy activists. Constructive deconstruction of existing orthodoxies and strategies must be encouraged. Activists serve as the eyes to the future for distracted or backward-looking leadership.

8. *Perspective is worth 50 IQ points.* Regrinding the lens through which the organization views the future makes everyone seem smarter. To face the Knowledge Age, each organization must: (a) identify the industry's conventions, (b) search for discontinuities that create opportunities to rewrite the industry's rules, (c) develop a deep understanding of the organization's core competencies, and (d) use this knowledge to seek revolutionary ideas. Innovation in the creation of strategy cannot occur without such a change in perspective.

9. *Top-down and bottom-up are not the alternatives.* To achieve diversity of perspective and unity of purpose, the strategy-making process must involve a deep diagonal slice of the organization—or several slices.

10. *You can't see the end from the beginning.* The futures revealed by such a planning process will always contain surprises and new vistas. These cannot be predicted at the beginning of the process. That is the point: true strategy leads in unsuspected directions that unlock unexpected opportunities.

Hamel's principles apply in all types of organizations, to all sectors and industries, but they are especially pertinent for higher education, whose dedication to incrementalism is legendary.

We are on the brink of the reinvention of the higher learning industry. A new learning industry for the 21st century is emerging from a fusion of parts of the education, information, and entertainment industries. This new learning industry will be global, K–99 (or even postpartum to post mortem), and much larger and more flexible than the current higher education industry. Strategic thinking for expeditionary products must begin with a clear vision of the transformative potential of this emerging learning industry.

Making the Blue Sky Meet the Road

Strategic thinking and vision are necessary but not sufficient. Armed with visions of the future, one must plan from the future backward. This process is called "making the blue sky meet the road." By pulling the future back to the present, one can clarify how to move toward that future.

A Knowledge Age vision can be used to gauge the gaps between personal and organizational competencies and those needed for the Knowledge Age. One can also identify elements of the current culture that hinder one's capacity to move forward and craft strategies to overcome them. Using this vision as a template, one can identify barriers to achieving the growth opportunities in Knowledge Age learning and strategies and initiatives for overcoming them.

One of the problems in identifying barriers and solutions is that they are analyzed in isolation. Barriers are interdependent and solutions are multifaceted and holistic. For example, the facts that faculty time is fully booked under the old paradigm and we do not typically use an investment paradigm (instead, we rely on "sweat equity") for developing new learning offerings are codependent. The solution: figure out how to raise larger resource pools for investment, focus faculty energies on expeditionary products that can attract investment, leverage faculty time through team development efforts, and mitigate risk through strategic alliances. Exhibit 1–3 illustrates a common set of barriers encountered by colleges and universities and a holistic set of interconnected strategies and initiatives to overcome them.

Experienced leaders understand how difficult it is to think about futures that may be dramatically different from extrapolations of today's experiences. Moreover, it is even more difficult to lead and stimulate an organization into thinking this way. It is especially difficult for many older staff, grounded in current paradigms, to think about different ways of being. Often, the feeling is "we can't get there from here."

Exhibit 1–3
BARRIERS TO ACHIEVING A KNOWLEDGE AGE VISION FOR LEARNING

Barriers Encountered	Examples of Strategies and Initiatives to Overcome Barriers
Time. Faculty time is fully booked under the old paradigm. The following two barriers—inadequate resources for new product development and failure to use an investment model—are corollaries.	Attract larger resource pools and use them to increase release time for new initiatives. Use multi- and trans-disciplinary teams of faculty, instructional development staff, and students to create new learning products.
Inadequate Resources for New Product Development. New learning products and initiatives are typically internally funded and conceived as incremental advances.	Craft revolutionary visions for learning products that attract strategic allies and investors. Appeal to larger markets. Use allies to migrate risk.
Failure to Use Investment Model. Due to the lack of resources and incremental orientation, most truly significant new learning product developments are fundamentally "sweat equity" propositions.	Decisively apply the investment model to new learning product development and the building of information technology (IT) infrastructure at all levels.
Evaluation and Promotion Criteria. Current evaluation criteria and promotion and tenure criteria do not sufficiently value or recognize the development of learningware and a focus on Knowledge Age learning	Begin the process of expanding the evaluation and promotion criteria to include Knowledge Age learning products. In the short term, engage faculty and staff at stages of their careers when they can participate without jeopardizing their future.
Prevailing Culture Unable to Act Responsively. Most academic cultures are unable to be nimble and are tied up in process.	Do not attempt to change the entire academic culture at once. Support units, programs, and initiatives that can be responsive. Create "skunk works" where new standards of responsiveness can be set in developing new learning products.
Coordinating Board and Accreditation Criteria. The current generation of performance measures is oriented toward traditional learning.	Begin the long-term process of changing, coordinating, and accrediting standards. Use strategic allies from business, the workplace, and the professionals.

(continued)

Exhibit 1–3
(Continued)

Barriers Encountered	Examples of Strategies and Initiatives to Overcome Barriers
Lack of Key Competencies. Faculty and administrative staff lack many of the basic competencies to develop Knowledge Age learning environments—vision, IT skills, academic culture, expeditionary product development, strategic alliances, and new financial models.	Use expeditionary product initiatives to build competencies and/or acquire competencies from strategic allies. To achieve optimal leverage, new initiatives should be expeditionary, engage supercharged strategic alliances, and change the financial paradigm.

When confronted with this sentiment, strategic thinking and planning in the future tense are necessary to break the logjam and plan from the future backward. When this happens, the feeling becomes, "We can't get there from here, but we can get here from there."

1.4 CHARTING ASSURED MIGRATION PATHS TO THE KNOWLEDGE AGE

Moving forward into the uncertain future requires a different kind of strategy and product planning. We must prepare for success under a variety of different futures. This requires charting a number of migration paths. To develop the competencies necessary to succeed in the Knowledge Age, we must use expeditionary development to develop and acquire six families of basic competencies. Revolutionary action without these competencies and an expeditionary approach has created some dramatic failures. Success requires a balance of revolutionary vision, evolutionary action, and expeditionary product development. In many ways, the new learning products and experiences—learningware—will follow the patterns and cadences of software development and Internet (Net) commerce. A synthesis of the experiences of the software and Net industries is provided to illustrate this development.

Preparing for Success under Multiple Scenarios

Knowledge Age planning is like climbing a mountain whose peak is shrouded in mist. Progress is measured by moving inexorably upward, positioning the expedition for future advances as the mist clears. In reality, the mist contains many scenarios for the future. We do not know which ones will occur, and in what measure. In reality, during the transition to the Knowledge Age, many different scenarios may all exist at the same time. It may take some time for learners to decisively select the most attractive scenarios. We can press for preferred futures, ones that best serve our institutions' interests. However, successful Knowledge Age planning requires maximizing our capacity to succeed under any potential future.

Such a situation should not be unfamiliar to American colleges and universities. The "traditional" institutions that form our higher education system already exist in a bewildering array of types: community colleges, liberal arts colleges, institutes of technology, and several kinds of university, all both public and private. Learners now can and do choose among these, but their learning options in the Knowledge Age will be multiplied manyfold.

Charting Assured Migration Paths

How can one talk about assured migration paths under such uncertain conditions? The essential point is that no single path or strategy will do. Nor will precise definitions of future killer applications likely suffice. The only sense of relative assurance that a learning enterprise can develop is by aggressively developing competencies that position the institution to take advantage of emerging opportunities before these opportunities become apparent to everyone.

The following steps will enable institutions to chart assured migration paths for the future of distributed learning:

1. *Generate shared visions of the future and continuously discuss with the community.* No single vision will do, but distributed learning is an excellent metaphor around which to focus strategic thinking. Leaders must provoke broad-ranging discussion of future visions. They must reframe the issues to focus on distributed learning, not current metaphors based on existing organizational structures and practices.

2. *Pull visions back to the present; identify and overcome barriers.* Current reward structures, promotion and tenure processes, allocation of faculty time, lack of investment for new product development, inability to leverage faculty time, lack of expertise in using teams to develop new products, and a host of other barriers prevent colleges and universities from capitalizing on the opportunities presented by distributed learning. Strategies must be developed to overcome these barriers.

3. *Redirect existing processes and launch new initiatives.* The emerging visions for distributed learning can be used to redirect existing processes—planning, budgeting and resource allocation,

infrastructure development, facilities planning, program review, promotion and tenure, institutional advancement, and others. New initiatives should be selected and funded on the basis of their capacity to build competencies that will enable achievement of the emerging vision.

4. *Use expeditionary approaches to new learning initiatives.* Expeditionary products are developed on a rapid prototype basis, with the expectation that they will be changed and improved continuously. They are intended to be used to collect information on an emerging market, to develop competencies in addressing that market, and to position the institution for major market opportunities that are not yet fully developed. Many of the tools needed to tap the emerging market are not yet even invented when the expeditionary product is first launched. Anyone who doubts the need for expeditionary marketing need only cite the list of technology-driven products that shot into the misty future like a laser beam—and missed.

5. *Develop the basic competencies for Knowledge Age products and services.* Expeditionary products are mechanisms for developing basic competencies. Many of these basic competencies will be acquired through strategic alliances. As these competencies are developed, they create the capacity for more decisive and successful action.

6. *Use strategic allies to acquire competencies, provide investment, and mitigate risk.* One cannot overemphasize the importance of strategic allies in a university's approach to Knowledge Age learning opportunities.

7. *Take decisive, even revolutionary, action when advisable.* At some point in the near future of emerging markets, it becomes possible to take decisive and even revolutionary action. The Apple Macintosh was the result of a series of expeditionary product developments that did not enjoy great success, but paved the way for the Macintosh.

Revolutionary Strategy, Evolutionary Action, Expeditionary Products

One of the frustrating ironies of Knowledge Age planning is the need to mix revolutionary vision with incremental action until basic competencies are developed, emerging markets take form, and new tools and techniques are developed. These competencies will enable decisive action on future programmatic opportunities as they become more clear and the state of the art of Knowledge Age tools develops.

But these incremental actions will be guided by revolutionary strategy and vision. Therefore, they will be more purposeful, commit greater pools of resources, and position institutions far more effectively than our normal habit of raging incrementalism, which is typically guided by past practices rather than future vision. When guided by revolutionary vision and strategy, learning enterprises can launch aggressive, evolutionary, and incremental actions that will develop assured migration paths and position the enterprise for even more decisive future action.

Expeditionary product development is central to this approach. It uses rapid prototypes of new learning products and experiences that are built rapidly, then modified continuously after being tested in the marketplace. These prototypes are characterized as "sticky" because they are able to collect information on learner needs and apply that information to immediate and continuous improvement. Sticky products are low-cost probes into the future. The self-correcting and self-adapting nature of sticky products suggests a biological metaphor for product development in the Knowledge Age.

Examples of Revolutionary Products That Failed

Truly revolutionary products seldom succeed in their first iterations. Technology-driven products often aim at the future and miss! Remember the following examples:

- Bell Laboratories' Picturephone—a mixture of video and voice technologies that found no market.

- Apple Computer's Newton—a breakthrough personal digital assistant.

- Control Data Corporation's PLATO[1]—a revolutionary approach to computer-based learning.

But these efforts were not totally wasted. Key aspects of these products were incorporated in new generations of sticky products, such as:

- Picturephone heralded new generations of videoconferencing tools that provide greater flexibility and capability than Picturephone.

---

[1]PLATO was originally created in the University of Illinois at Urbana-Champaign and provides an early example of university-industry partnering.

- Newton technology and concepts are incorporated in a new generation of digital assistants and durable laptop devices for kids.

- PLATO is being offered on-line by Magellan University and also heralds the arrival of a new generation of Web-based tools.

The software industry abounds with examples of the wisdom of expeditionary, sticky products. Clearly, most software products use initial releases as expeditionary approaches, not just to test the market but also to work out performance issues.

Learningware in the Image of Software and Net Commerce

The growth opportunities for learning in the Knowledge Age will require the development of a new learningware/learning architecture industry. New practices and competencies are required to shape this new industry. The next generations of learningware products will follow the patterns and cadences of the software industry much more than the patterns of traditional academic products (e.g., the textbook publishing industry).

The notion of expeditionary marketing has emerged in the 1990s as corporate growth has shifted from companies that are achieving cost and quality advantages in well-defined existing markets to those that are building and dominating fundamentally new markets characterized by rapid change and technological development (Hamel and Prahalad 1991). To identify and capitalize on new opportunities, companies developed the capacity to create products serving genuinely new needs and to treat those products as prototypes to be refined in the marketplace. Laptop computers, minivans, and wireless communications have demonstrated the shift from the old product logic to a new mindset. See Exhibit 1–4.

The new product mindset focuses on opportunities and creating new competitive space. It recognizes that customers must be led in establishing genuinely new products that they have not experienced, but also knows that the new prototypes must be continuously assessed and modified. The new products are functionality-driven. Maximizing the success rate is not as important as maximizing the learning from new products. Investment and persistence are necessary to demonstrate commitment.

The accelerating pace of change in the 1990s has developed these principles further. A 1997 survey of companies in the computer industry revealed critical success factors for product development in an atmosphere of continuous change (Brown and Eisenhardt 1997).

Put simply, successful companies were able to:

- Plan and launch rapid prototype products that serve as low-cost probes into the future

Exhibit 1–4
PRODUCT MINDSET

The Old Product Logic	The New Product Mindset
• Served markets	• Opportunity horizons
• Defending today's business	• Creating new competitive space
• Following customers	• Leading customers
• Periodic assessment	• Continuous assessment and feedback
• Product-driven	• Functionality-driven
• Maximizing the success rate of new products	• Maximizing the learning from new products
• Commitment reflected in investment	• Commitment reflected in persistence

Source: Adapted from Hamel and Prahalad, 1991

- Assess and communicate success and acceptance and continuously reshape the products and their derivatives

- Create a rhythmically choreographed transition from present to future

Put another way, the most successful companies are not those that plan for two years for products that will last for five. Rather, success goes to those who rapid-prototype a product in three months, then use continuous assessment and improvement to create changed and derivative products that evolve into cutting-edge applications. Five years after introduction, the product is dramatically different than when introduced.

The new learningware industry will follow these patterns and cadences, not those of the traditional learning industry. It will also be influenced by the economics of Net commerce. One of the basic competencies that will be needed in the Knowledge Age is the capacity to understand the new life cycles, rhythms, and economics of learningware and Net commerce.

1.5 BASIC COMPETENCIES FOR THE KNOWLEDGE AGE

To be successful in the world of Knowledge Age learning, learning enterprises will need to develop or acquire six families of basic competencies (see Exhibit 1–5). These are not "core" competencies, which are the core distinguishing characteristics of an enterprise. Basic competencies can be learned or developed internally, or acquired through strategic alliances. The first three families of basic competencies are contextual. The last three are a combination that will be present in successful Knowledge Age ventures. Many of the basic competencies needed for Knowledge Age learning will require strategic alliances with other colleges and universities, other learning enterprises, educational management organizations, training and development providers, instructional media companies, telecommunications and technology companies, and other participants.

New Approaches to Leadership, Strategy, and Vision

Campus leaders need to engage in genuine strategic thinking that plans backward from the future, challenging our prevailing assumptions about the higher education industry. To support this effort, campus leaders must engage their campus communities—faculty, staff, and other stakeholders—in dialogues about the future of higher learning in the Knowledge Age. This is an ongoing process, not a one-time conversation or campus convocation. Broad-based participatory discussions must accompany new initiatives and redirection of existing programs and processes to build the competencies to thrive in the Knowledge Age.

Exhibit 1–5
BASIC COMPETENCIES FOR THE KNOWLEDGE AGE

Basic Competencies	Primary Application
New Approaches to Leadership, Vision, and Strategy	• Critical contextual competency for the successful learning enterprise. Essential for breakthrough products.
IT and Learning Infrastructure and Skills	• Critical contextual competency for the successful learning enterprise. Essential for breakthrough products.
Changing the Academic Culture	• Critical contextual competency. Essential for breakthrough products.
New Types of Learning Products, Services, and Interactions	• Element of breakthrough products.
New Financial Paradigms	• Element of breakthrough products.
Supercharged Strategic Alliances	• Element of breakthrough products.

Symbols, metaphors, and new ways of thinking about the future are key. Escape the boundaries of old ideas and organizational structures by using concepts like "distributed learning" that span all boundaries and structures.

Strategy innovation will be one of the defining new competencies of successful Knowledge Age colleges and universities. Their leaders must be able to craft new strategies that position their programs for success in a new "knowledge and learning industry" that is emerging from the fusion of education, entertainment, and information.

IT, Learning Infrastructure, and Skills

To provide attractive alternatives to distributed learning offerings from other institutions and new competitors, it will be necessary for colleges and universities to invest not only in information technology (IT) infrastructure, but also in faculty and staff user skills, to develop a learning infrastructure of virtual learning tools and interactivity that can be fused with traditional on-campus learning. Most campuses will need to rely on strategic alliances with other institutions, new learning providers, and others to acquire learning infrastructure competencies.

Changing the Academic Culture

To compete in the Knowledge Age, colleges and universities must establish academic cultures capable of spawning learning products, services, and experiences that meet Knowledge Age standards of timeliness, responsiveness, customization, coherence, and convenience. In most institutions, changing the entire academic culture is not practical. It is better to target particular academic units or special institutes, such as continuing education, professional education, distance learning, and/or creative undergraduate programs. Establish these units as "skunk works" or incubators where new products and services can be developed, then transfer the organizational DNA to other parts of the institution.

New Types of Learning Products, Services, and Interactions

To be competitive in the Knowledge Age learning environment, even traditional colleges and universities will need to provide access to new learning tools and experiences. These will include virtual variations on traditional learning, new approaches to certification of mastery and provision of credit for prior learning, creation of interactivity-centered learning models, and customizing of learning experiences to individual needs.

One of us has argued elsewhere (Langenberg 1997) that degrees and diplomas are obsolete and that they will eventually be displaced by much finer-grained certifications of mastery (like Scout merit badges or the elements of an academic's curriculum vitae). These will be better adapted to the circumstances of perpetual learners, who will learn from many different institutions, sequentially or simultaneously, and according to the needs of their employers. This may well require the development of a national or even international system of common academic currency, not to mention radical changes in our systems for certifying and accrediting institutions.

Institutions cannot acquire these competencies on their own. Strategic alliances with a wide range of potential partners must be considered: other colleges and universities, telecommunications and technology companies, corporate and proprietary learning providers, content packagers/repackagers, content distributors, learning center operators, entertainment companies, assessment specialists, and other significant players.

New Financial Paradigms

One of the most significant new competencies will be the capacity to re-align the financial paradigms for higher learning with the new realities of the Knowledge Age. This realignment should encompass variations on the following themes:

- Make a significant proportion of IT infrastructure an investment, creating new sources of revenue to assure the continuing enhancement of IT and learning infrastructure.

- Treat the development of new Knowledge Age products and services as investments, using strategic allies and investors to create investment pools and mitigate the risk of new program development.

- Create virtual commerce capabilities so the use of learning tools and access to information and knowledge can be paid for on-line, on a pay-for-use basis.

- Tap new sources of revenue relating to Knowledge Age learning: new markets for virtualized and atomized versions of learning products, new products and services for existing markets, innovative fund-raising tied to Knowledge Age learning initiatives, and new user fees for technology-based services.

- Reduce the cost and price to students for particular learning experiences by giving credit for competencies acquired elsewhere, eliminating unnecessary lock-step learning, reducing time-to-degree and delays due to course unavailability, and introducing other mechanisms to accelerate the learning experience.

■ Create opportunities for perpetual learning and ongoing mentorship relationships between faculty and graduates, leading to continuous active learning and revenue streams.

Competition and consumer resistance will drive down the price the market will bear for learning experiences. This effect will be mitigated at iconographic institutions, where social positions and selection are as important to price as learning value. Educators should remember that the period immediately preceding major industry adjustments is often the most successful and lucrative period for providers. This is just before more nimble and resourceful competitors change the patterns in the industry.

To survive this paradigm adjustment, institutions must be prepared to grow, capitalizing on the opportunities provided by Knowledge Age learning.

Supercharged Strategic Alliances

A wave of new strategic alliances is beginning to ripple through higher learning. These alliances are focusing on building infrastructure, developing Knowledge Age products and services, and creating new financial paradigms—all at the same time. This new breed of alliances will involve a wide range of participants: other institutions, other learning providers, technology companies, and employers requiring learning brokers. In many of these strategic alliances, the traditional institution will not be the dominant member.

Colleges and universities should become accustomed to participating in learning ventures where they do not control the entire value chain. They must acquire access to these competencies if they are to succeed in the world of the Knowledge Age learner. Those that do not will find themselves at the mercy of a readjusting marketplace.

1.6   EXAMPLES OF BREAKTHROUGH INITIATIVES

A number of learning enterprises have developed breakthough learning initiatives that combine expeditionary products, supercharged strategic alliances, and new financial paradigms. A variety of examples illustrate how these new models are emerging today:

■ Instructional Management System, National Learning Infrastructure

- Western Governors University

- University of Maryland University College

- The Seamless Learning System

- University System of Maryland

- Cyberschool Initiative, Virginia Tech

- New Century College, George Mason University

- University of Wisconsin Learning Innovations

The following descriptions describe these new models, some in relative detail, others more generally. These models will create more responsive capabilities that will be reflected in dramatically changing learning product platforms in the future.

Instructional Management System, National Learning Infrastructure Initiative

Under the auspices of Educom's National Learning Infrastructure Initiative (NLII), the Instructional Management System (IMS) has been launched to advance the development environment for instructional software tools. Although use of the World Wide Web/Java environment is increasing standardization of platforms and operating systems, a larger issue remains unresolved: managing the learning process and providing a framework within which individual software objects, modules, or atoms of content can be integrated. The IMS project was launched to establish higher order standards to address these requirements and a set of tools to create, access, and manage the use of Web-based instructional software.

The IMS project will provide a set of standards, tools to provide these services, proof-of-concept, and a process for engaging interested parties in participating in the project. The project will enable a variety of participants to integrate existing instructional applications into the IMS, including products developed at the Institute for Academic Technology (IAT) at the University of North Carolina, materials developed as part of Project Synergy at Miami Dade Community College, and Web-based applications developed with National Science Foundation/National Institute of Education funding at other institutions.

The project is being managed by the California State University (CSU) Instructional Technology Development Institute. CSU, IAT, and the University of Michigan will develop the standards and prototype tools that constitute the IMS. A variety of commercial organizations are partners in the IMS, including publishing houses, hardware firms, and software companies. The prototype will be deployed within institutions affiliated with the partnership in 1998. A description of IMS's current status is available at http://www.imsproject.org.

Expeditionary Development. The IMS initiative is strongly expeditionary. Its aim is to develop a prototype set of standards, tools, and applications that demonstrate the concept. These prototypes will be tested among IMS partners in 1998 and deployed more broadly in 1999. Based on assessment of the effectiveness of the IMS, the project team will develop and release version 2.0 of the IMS specifications and push for broad adoption of the specifications. To be successful, these standards and tools should be continuously tuned to reflect feedback and newly emerging applications needs.

This initiative is targeted at stimulating the rapid development of a learningware industry that will create scalable software products, modules, atoms of content, simulations, and other interactivity-based learning support materials. This industry will be global and highly competitive. By their very nature, these products will have to be expeditionary, capturing feedback on effectiveness and using it to continuously improve the products and generate new derivatives.

Financial Investment.   From its inception IMS deployed an investment model. Venture partners contributed a substantial pool of resources to fund the initiative. New partners joined for a membership fee of $50,000. The financial support for the project has allowed rapid development of the prototype standards and tools, and has created commitment from the venture partners.

Supercharged Strategic Alliances.   IMS started with a core group of institutional and industry partners. The strategic importance of the project has generated substantial interest in the emerging learning industry and has attracted a variety of key players, including the United States Department of Defense and several corporate learning divisions of major corporations. This will assure that the standards and tools developed through IMS set the standards for the entire learning industry, not just traditional educational institutions. The strategic importance of their inclusion cannot be overstated.

Sources of Value in Five to Seven Years.   IMS's great promise and value is to establish an open standard for the emerging learningware industry, thereby avoiding the years of squabbling among competing proprietary standards that characterized earlier technology introductions (such as computer operating system and telecommunication standards). This will encourage rapid development of the learningware industry by providing standards and examples of how to create scalable software products, attracting venture capital to this development and encouraging the forging of alliances. IMS's great contribution will be the development of this industry and the benefits that will flow to learners, learning agents, developers, and other participants.

How will IMS develop over time? What will be the high-value-added components for which participants will pay a premium? Only time will tell. If experience is any guide, the core service provided by IMS will quickly become a commodity. Increasingly powerful and higher-level learning management, learning agent services, and market research based on use of IMS may be among the high-value-added services for which users will pay premiums.

Western Governors University

The governors of the Western states launched the Western Governors University (WGU) out of frustration with the inability of educational leaders to respond with new learning strategies to meet the demographically driven coming tidal waves of learners in the West. The high inertia of existing institutional models, structures, and leadership dramatized the need for boundary-busting action, and the governors were only too willing to comply.

The Western Governors University was established with the following design principles (Johnstone and Jones 1997):

- The institution will be market-oriented and client-centered.

- WGU will be degree-granting and accredited by the appropriate academic associations.

- The institution will use a distributed teaching faculty coming from public and private higher education and private industry.

- The sharing of regional courses will achieve cost-effectiveness and promote intra- and interstate resource sharing.

- WGU will require member states to develop local learning centers to serve as technology access points and physical locations for proctoring exams and other functions.

The governors also recommended that WGU focus on those areas where it could add value to existing institutions and capacity, leading to the following characteristics:

- Link employers and academic institutions in setting skills standards, connecting individuals and assessment providers, and certifying competence in several domains of learning—transferable skills, vocational skills, general academic knowledge, and specific disciplinary knowledge.

- Link individuals with educational providers who can meet learners' requirements regarding time, place, and content.

- Provide support services and reduce barriers to access.

- Acquire or pool financial resources necessary to develop learning and assessment tools in high-priority areas where the market has not responded.

- Provide degrees and certificates to individuals demonstrating competencies.

The staff working on this is sorting through the issues relating to staffing and roles of faculty, student support, financing, and other factors. The most critical tools of the WGU are the competency-based certifications and the Web-based smart catalog/advisor.

Expeditionary Development.   The WGU is the archetypical expeditionary product. Its design principles were developed to change many of the established principles of the traditional education paradigm. The university is designed to take advantage of changes in learning and assessment technology, as they emerge. Its core services of competency assessment and navigation/advising position WGU to serve as learning agent and assessment agent for learners. WGU can bundle and access "best of breed" learning experiences and services from whatever sources emerge. Its work with learners and providers will continually identify new permutations and needs to be addressed.

WGU staff have a very real sense that the learning world is changing rapidly—and that the products and services they are developing for rollout must be more adaptive than has previously been experienced. They also have an appreciation for the changing value equation.

Financial Investment.   WGU was developed using an investment model. Its initial funding support from the Western governors is being supplemented by investment capital in a variety of forms. Over time, WGU will need to establish a viable financial paradigm for virtual learning materials.

Supercharged Strategic Alliances.   By its design, WGU must seek and establish strategic alliances with assessment providers, faculty, and learning providers. However, its alliance-generating capacities have proven even greater. The announcement of WGU and its design have prompted expressions of interest from a great variety of universities, ranging from the Open University in the United Kingdom to universities in Asia, New Zealand, Australia, and elsewhere.

Sources of Value in Five to Ten Years.   It is likely that WGU and other virtual universities will follow an expeditionary path over the next five to ten years, if they prove sufficiently adaptive to be successful. The brokering of purely virtual learning experiences will not be their cutting-edge application. The greatest value of WGU, and its greatest source of revenues, is likely to be in the following areas:

- Providing certification of mastery for learning achieved anywhere (in strategic alliance with major assessment providers or corporate learning enterprises)

- Maintaining skills and competency banks for learners all over the globe (through strategic alliances)

- Brokering a variety of virtualized, atomized, and transformed learning materials and services that are part of distributed learning environments on campuses worldwide

- Opening up strategic alliances with international colleges and universities wishing to be partners in virtual or distributed learning enterprises

- Opening up strategic alliances with the emerging Knowledge Age learning industry

- Providing a vehicle for creating distributed learning services that can be deployed to raise standards in K–12 education

- Stimulating the development of a community learning center industry and an industry of residential living/learning environments in communities across the nation

These derivative products may be the real cutting-edge applications.

University of Maryland University College

The University of Maryland University College (UMUC) was founded 50 years ago as the continuing adult education unit of the University of Maryland. In 1970 it became an independent constituent institution of what is now the University of Maryland (USM).

University College is the USM's skunk works. Through most of its existence it has been the principal provider of postsecondary education to U.S. military personnel overseas. This has endowed it with a flexibility and adaptability foreign to traditional institutions, including its 10 degree-granting sisters in the USM. University College knows how to respond when many of its students suddenly depart in mid-term, as did a large portion of its European Division enrollment in the autumn of 1990 (to Saudi Arabia to prepare for Operation Desert Storm). Its faculty are used to teaching classes in which every student comes armed with an assault rifle.

University College has developed many characteristics that make it an apt pilot for higher education's journey into the Knowledge Age. During most of its life it has received no state funding whatsoever. It has therefore been compelled to operate like a for-profit not-for-profit. It has only a small cadre of full-time faculty, most of whom double as academic program managers. Most of its faculty are professionals otherwise employed in positions related to the subjects they teach. There are no tenured or tenure-track faculty. University College has little physical infrastructure. There is a headquarters building, but most of its classes are held in facilities owned by others (e.g., industries, other institutions of the USM, community colleges, leased spaces, and military bases). As its president is fond of saying, "We hold school in other peoples' school houses." There is no library and no football team. University College's programs focus on areas of primary interest to working adults, like management and technology. University College is adaptable. It has been known to design and deliver a new academic program to client specifications within just a few weeks. And University College thinks globally. Former Chairman of the Joint Chiefs of Staff, General Lyman Lemnitzer, at a University College commencement, once adapted a sobriquet of the former British Empire to "The sun never sets on the University of Maryland." That remains true to this day. Last year, University College enrolled students on all seven continents, including one at McMurdo Station in Antarctica who was taking a course with a professor based in Okinawa. (Technically, General Lemnitzer was wrong. That student's sun had set for a period of several months.)

Expeditionary Development.   On its global historical base of experience, University College is rapidly building a global virtual university. It has internally developed a software system designed to support a complete virtual university (not simply a virtual classroom). This system (called TYCHO, after Tycho Brahe, the Danish astronomer whose work helped drive the scientific transition from the Middle Ages to the Renaissance and the Enlightenment) provides all the necessary student services and library functions needed by remotely located students, in addition to the necessary classroom functions. Though University College has heretofore relied mainly on site-based delivery of its programs, it is moving quickly into cyberspace. It now has more than a dozen complete baccalaurate and master's programs available on the World Wide Web (WWW), and expects that almost all of its programs will be Web-accessible by the turn of the millennium. These programs now have enrolled students in all 50 American states. University College expects that about half of its state-side students will be virtual within several years.

Financial Investment.   University College has always operated using an investment model, because it has had to. So far, its capital has been mostly internally generated, but it is now actively seeking external partners.

Supercharged Strategic Alliances.   University College's primary strategic partner has historically been the U.S. Department of Defense. The importance of that strategic alliance cannot be overestimated. It has substantially shaped the culture and character of the institution. But there are others. For example, University College offers an American-style master's degree in management in collaboration with the Universities of Irkutsk and Vladivostok in Siberia. Closer (much closer) to home, it has established so-called "2+2" partnerships with several Maryland community colleges that will make University College baccalaureate programs available at the community colleges. In mid-1998 it expects to launch a joint enterprise with a private partner that will expand its civilian site-based program delivery outside of Maryland and, eventually perhaps, worldwise.

Sources of Value in Five to Ten Years.   University College's future path is intrinsically expeditionary. It builds on a solid historical base, but some of its current initiatives are far from risk-free. Its challenge will be to maintain and enhance its demonstrated adaptability, to learn from its early experiences, and thus to succeed. If it does, it will open up a global market of breathtaking magnitude. The greater hope is that its more conventional and traditional sister institutions in the University System of Maryland can be induced to follow along on the trail University College is pioneering. Unfortunately, some of them may be overly conscious of the canonical definition of a *pioneer*: "It's that guy face down in the mud with the arrows in his back."

The Seamless Learning System

Another, broader kind of academic strategic alliance is now emerging in several states. In Maryland it is called the Partnership for Teaching and Learning K–16, or the "K–16 Partnership" for short. Unlike the alliances envisioned elsewhere in this chapter, these K–16 partnerships are alliances of higher education and elementary- and secondary-education systems at the state level. These alliances also often include organizations representing the business community's commitment to elementary- and secondary-school reform.

The fundamental notion underlying such alliances is that the entire education system—elementary through postsecondary—is one strongly coupled system that ought to be (but now is not) completely seamless. The initial focus is usually reform of the K–12 system through standards-based assessment of school and student performance, aided by higher education. The most casual consideration of this issue, however, reveals that K–12 reform must necessarily be accompanied by higher education reform, including realignment of admissions criteria, radical reform of teacher education, and, ultimately, performance-based certification of mastery at all postsecondary levels. These therefore also become objectives of such K–16 partnerships.

A little reflection will convince the reader that all of the ideas presented earlier in this chapter are directly applicable to these K–16 strategic alliances. Though we talk about K–16, we really mean a learning industry that is K–99, postpartum to post mortem. To give just one example, it is estimated that in the next decade American schools will need to hire 2 million new teachers. At present rates, our colleges and universities will graduate about 1 million. Moreover, many of the teachers now teaching in our schools are not academically qualified to do so; in some schools the proportion of unqualified teachers reaches 40 percent. We thus face not only a huge challenge in preparing new teachers, but also an equally large challenge in qualifying existing teachers. If ever there was a situation where expeditionary strategy was called for, this is it.

Expeditionary Development.   This is what the K–16 partnerships now under development in a few states are all about.

Financial Investment.   Several K–16 partnerships have been the beneficiaries of substantial investment by their states and school systems; several have not—yet. But public concern about the performance of the public schools is such that it seems likely that such partnerships will become the focus of substantial public (and perhaps private) investment, once they are recognized as the expeditionary strategic movements they really are.

Sources of Value in Five to Ten Years.   The ultimate goal of K–16 strategic alliances is to make the entire American learning system the envy of the world, as its higher education component is, rather than the national embarrassment that its K–12 component now is. That goal cannot be reached in a mere five to ten years, but it ought to be possible to make substantial progress toward it.

University System of Maryland

In addition to the two foregoing examples, the University System of Maryland has been engaged for nearly a decade in striving to become a real system: a family of ten universities, one college, and two research and service institutions that truly functions as a strongly interacting open system whose performance is much more than a simple sum of the performances of its constituent parts. It has had many successes, but many more await it. It has provided technological and management infrastructures that now permit its institutions to share their library resources statewide; to offer joint graduate programs in which much of the instruction is done via an interactive video network; and to offer academic programs in many areas of the state from one institution teaching on the turf of another. Student transfers among community colleges and four-year colleges are now electronically facilitated on-line, from initial counseling through transcript transfer and electronic application. But there is still plenty of room for further expeditionary strategy.

Cyberschool Initiative, Virginia Tech

Virginia Tech is located in Blacksburg, Virginia, the home of the Blacksburg Electronic Village (BEV). Despite its rural and remote location, Blacksburg enjoys the highest level of Internet usage of any town or city in the United States. Information about the BEV and the Cyberschool Initiative can be found at www.bev.net and www.vt.edu.

One of the most significant initiatives launched by Virginia Tech is its Cyberschool, a fusion of computer-interactive classroom methodologies, traditional classroom practice, advanced multimedia programs, and distance learning. It was conceptualized as a virtual campus, breaking the mold of credit for contact and thereby meeting the needs of a diverse student body over the next decade and beyond. It was a response to the necessity of teaching more students with no additional resources in terms of the number of faculty and classroom buildings.

The Cyberschool Initiative includes a number of interconnected facets:

- Faculty training and development. Beginning with the College of Arts and Sciences, faculty cohorts of 300 or more were given hands-on training in the use of on-line tools and the infusion of technology into learning. Over a three- to four-year period, all faculty will be put through this experience.

- Creation of virtual classes. A variety of virtual learning environments have been created in many academic disciplines. These classes have been used to assess and refine virtual approaches.

- Development of learningware snippets. Substantial effort has been invested in the development of learningware tools for use at Virginia Tech and in other learning settings. Many of these are learningware "snippets"—less than a full course or even a full one-hour class session—that many faculty will be comfortable integrating into their class activities.

- Continuous improvement and innovation. The virtual classes, learningware development, and activities of individual faculty are under constant evaluation and improvement. The virtual classes have been reshaped continuously, creating a variety of distributed learning experiences.

- Outreach to other learning settings. The Cyberschool Initiative is positioning Virginia Tech to support distributed learning across the Commonwealth of Virginia and to be a thought leader for other schools. It is also positioning Tech to be a major player in the emerging learningware industry, nationally and even globally.

This initiative demonstrates the establishment of a migration path to develop or acquire all of the basic competencies for Knowledge Age products. Clearly, Virginia Tech's leaders have demonstrated vision and commitment to new strategy. Although Tech has been a leader in IT infrastructure, this initiative also reveals a substantial commitment to technology, faculty, and learningware infrastructure. As for cultural change, by training all faculty and inviting them to integrate technology into learning and research, the institution is attempting pervasive cultural change. The most ambitious virtual and distributed learning initiatives, in contrast, serve as something of a "skunk works" of innovation.

Expeditionary Development. The Cyberschool Initiative is more than just a virtual learning initiative. It is serving as an expeditionary initiative to create distributed learning capabilities on the Blacksburg campus and in other learning settings. These distributed learning capabilities are continuously changing.

New Financial Paradigm. There are three signal characteristics that differentiate Virginia Tech's financial paradigm for technology development: strategic alliances, substantial investment, and new revenue streams. The Cyberschool Initiative was preceded by the BEV, made possible by a substantial strategic alliance between Virginia Tech, the Town of Blacksburg, and Bell Atlantic. Significant resources were invested in BEV. The university put $10 million of its own resources into Cyberschool and related items, and it is counting on significant new revenue streams in the future from its participation in distributed learning environments.

Supercharged Strategic Alliances. The strategic alliance to create BEV has been a critical factor in these developments. As Tech is creating more virtual and distributed learningware tools, it is entering into arrangements with many publishers and developers.

Sources of Value in Five to Ten Years. Virginia Tech's Cyberschool Initiative and related activities are building its competencies for participating in Knowledge Age learning. These will yield substantial opportunities five to ten years in the future. Rather than being a single expeditionary initiative, Virginia Tech's investment represents a broad and diverse commitment to building new competencies that can be used to capitalize on the new opportunities that emerge.

New Century College, George Mason University

New Century College (NCC) is an innovative program where students create their own self-paced degree programs and extensively apply the tools of Knowledge Age scholarship. NCC has no faculty of its own; it draws its faculty from other academic departments and selects the faculty who are committed to its distinctive approach to learning. George Mason University (GMU) is well known for creating innovative programs and cultures.

NCC involves students in student-centered learning communities from their first semester on campus. Faculty teach in teams and the intensity and pattern of interaction between students and faculty vary over the course of the semester. NCC is seen as a work in progress from which insights will spread throughout the university. It will build the following competencies:

- Leadership in creating learner-centered communities
- A responsive, innovative, continuously improving academic culture, drawing faculty from other academic units
- Faculty and student skills in developing technology-enabled learning communities
- An expeditionary approach to the NCC's program

- A new financial model for undergraduate instruction, using learning communities rather than large lecture sections

More about the New Century Program can be located at www.gmu.edu.

University of Wisconsin Learning Innovations

The University of Wisconsin (UW) is an internationally recognized leader in continuing education, cooperative extension, distance education, public radio and television, and other outreach activities. Even so, UW has found it difficult to mobilize and leverage its considerable competencies and resources to address the needs and market opportunities in distributed learning. The "coefficient of friction" associated with attempting rapid change within existing academic cultures has been a problem, even in units such as Continuing Education, which are more adaptive than most. The restrictions associated with state procurement and accountability standards have made expeditionary program development difficult.

The UW Regents approved the creation of UW Learning Innovations (UWLI), a subsidiary unit with an attached 501(c)(3) corporation, to address this opportunity. Michael Offerman, UW-Extension's Dean of Continuing Education, will lead UWLI. It will serve as a utility, enabling faculty throughout the UW system to develop, market, and distribute learning products and services worldwide through technology. Its aim is to set new standards of responsiveness, competitiveness, timeliness, and customization in the development of learning products and services.

1.7 CONCLUSION

Learning will be a substantial growth industry in the Knowledge Age. The new learning industry will be global, K–99, and highly responsive. It will be necessary for learning products and services to meet new and higher standards of timeliness, coherence, and customization. These products will change rapidly and be expeditionary in nature.

Who will be the leaders in this new industry? The history of innovation and industry realignment suggests that innovative leadership does not come from leaders under the existing paradigms. New competitors and thought leaders are emerging.

Whether they are new thought leaders or existing learning providers, the successful learning enterprise in the Knowledge Age will deploy expeditionary strategy and product development. This will be a basic competency for the Knowledge Age.

SOURCES AND SUGGESTED READINGS

Armstrong, Steve, Gail Thompson, and Sally Brown. *Facing Up to Radical Changes in Universities and Colleges*. London: Kogan Page Limited, 1997.

Botkin, James, and Stan Davis. *The Monster under the Bed: How Business Is Mastering the Opportunity of Knowledge for Profit*. New York: Simon & Schuster, 1994.

Brown, John Seeley, and P. Duguid. "Universities in the Digital Age." *Change* 28, no. 3 (1996): 1–8.

Brown, Shona L., and Kathleen M. Eisenhardt. "The Art of Continuous Change Linking Complexity Theory and Time-Paced Evolution in Continuously Shifting Organizations." *Administrative Science Quarterly* 42, no. 1 (March 1997): 1–34.

Cronin, Blaise, and Tom Duffy. *Distributed Education and Indiana University*. Working Paper No. 1: Content, Trends, Assumptions, Distance Education Advisory Committee.

Daniel, John S. *Mega-universities and Knowledge Media*. London: Kogan Page Limited, 1997.

De Geus, Arie. *The Living Company*. Cambridge: Harvard Business School Press, 1997.

Denning, Peter J. "Business Designs for the New University," *Educom Review* (November 1996): 20–30.

———. "How We Will Learn." In *Beyond Calculation: The Next Fifty Years of Computing*. New York: Springer-Verlag, 1997.

Drucker, Peter. "The Age of Social Transformation," *Atlantic Monthly* (November 1994): 53–80.

Graves, William H. "Free Trade in Higher Education: The Meta-University." Internet posted article, JALN Homepage.

Hamel, Gary. "Killer Strategies That Make Shareholders Rich." *Fortune*, June 23, 1997, pp. 70–84.

———. "Strategy as Revolution." *Harvard Business Review* (July/August 1996): 66–72.

Hamel, Gary, and C.K. Prahalad. *Competing for the Future*. Cambridge: Harvard Business School Press, 1994.

———. "Corporate Imagination and Expeditionary Marketing." *Harvard Business Review* (July/August 1991).

Handy, Charles. *The Age of Paradox*. Cambridge: Harvard Business School Press, 1994.

———. *The Age of Unreason*. Cambridge: Harvard Business School Press, 1989.

Heselbein, Frances, Marshall Goldsmith, and Richard Beckhard. *The Leader of the Future*. San Francisco: Jossey-Bass Drucker Foundation, 1996.

James, Jennifer. *Thinking in the Future Tense: Leadership Skills for the New Age*. New York: Simon & Schuster, 1996.

Johnstone, Sally M., and Dennis Jones. "New Higher Education Trends Reflected in the Design of the Western Governors University." *On the Horizon* (November/December 1997): 8–11.

Kotter, John P. *Leading Change*. Cambridge: Harvard Business School Press, 1996.

Langenberg, Donald N. "Degrees and Diplomas Are Obsolescent." *Chronicle of Higher Education* (September 12, 1997): A64.

Lanham, Ernest A. *The Electronic Word: Democracy, Technology and the Arts*. Chicago: The University of Chicago Press, 1993.

Noam, Eli. "Electronics and the Dim Future of the University." *Science* 270 (Oct. 13, 1995): 247–249.

Nonaka, Ikujiro and Hirotaka Takeuchi. *The Knowledge-Creating Company*. New York: Oxford University Press, 1995.

Norris, Donald M. *Revolutionary Strategy for the Knowledge Age*. Ann Arbor, Mich.: Society for College and University Planning, 1997.

———. "The Significance of Virtual Universities." *On the Horizon* (November/December 1997): 14–16.

Norris, Donald M., and Michael G. Dolence. *Transforming Higher Education: A Vision for Learning in the 21st Century*. Ann Arbor, Mich.: Society for College and University Planning, 1995.

Norris, Donald M., and Theodore Roosevelt Malloch. *Unleashing the Power of Perpetual Learning*. Ann Arbor, Mich.: Society for College and University Planning, 1997.

O'Bannion, Terry. *A Learning Vision for the 21st Century*. Washington, D.C.: American Council on Education and American Association of Community Colleges, 1997.

Oblinger, Diana G., and Sean C. Rush, eds. *The Learning Revolution*. Boston: Anker Publishing, 1997.

Ohmae, Kenichi. *The Mind of the Strategist*. New York: Penguin Books, 1984.

Penzias, Arno. *Digital Harmony: Business, Technology, and Life After Paperwork*. New York: Harper Business, 1995.

Perelman, Lewis. *School's Out: A Radical New Formula for the Revitalization of America's Educational System*. New York: Avon Books, 1992.

Rich, Ben, and Leo Janos. *Skunk Works*. New York: Little, Brown & Company, 1994.

Sveiby, Karl Erik. *The New Organizational Wealth*. San Francisco: Berrett-Koehler Publishers, 1997.

Tapscott, Don. *The Digital Economy*. New York: McGraw-Hill, 1995.

Treacy, Michael, and Fred Wiersema. *The Discipline of Market Leaders*. New York: Addison-Wesley, 1995.

Twigg, Carol. *Academic Productivity: The Case for Educational Software.* Washington, D.C.: EDUCOM, 1996.

———. *A Need for a National Learning Infrastructure.* Washington, D.C.: EDUCOM, 1995.

Twigg, Carol, and Diana Oblinger. *Virtual Universities.* Washington, D.C., EDUCOM, 1997.

PART TWO

Important Lessons About Being Expeditionary

The Business End of the One-to-One Future in Learning and Credentialing

DON PEPPERS

Partner
Marketing 1 to 1/Peppers and Rogers Group

MARTHA ROGERS, PH.D.

Partner
Marketing 1 to 1/Peppers and Rogers Group

2.1   INTRODUCTION

The controversy that is raging about higher education often focuses on "experience"—a comparison of the four-year resident campus to an efficient on-line knowledge transfer. It is impossible to determine which is "better" out of a specific context. For the middle-class high school graduate, the traditional experience may offer life learning as well as a college diploma. To the middle-aged mother of three looking to improve her career choices, the most efficient knowledge transfer is her best bet. In every context, experience is tempered by a consideration of cost and value. Much of the future direction of higher education will be determined by plain old money.

2.2   WHAT TYPE OF LEARNING EXPERIENCE IS BEST?

You can spend the night at the Ritz, or a bed and breakfast, or a Red Roof Inn, or your own apartment. All of them will get you through the night. But they vary in price, efficiency, status, geographic availability, and the necessity for reservations—among other things. A college education is increasingly less relevant than lifelong learning, as the lines blur among degrees, courses, classes, and seminars and the motivation for attendance becomes more and more pragmatic. (For those who decry the loss of "education" this change represents, it may be more or less comforting to realize that the shift from art to practicality is already a *fait accompli*—of the 1 million bachelor's degrees awarded in 1991, only 7,300 were in philosophy and religion, yet over 250,000 were in business.[1] Already, academic credentialing is primarily used to prepare for work.)

Lew Perelman compares a luxurious steamship with a basic jet plane. Which is better? According to Perelman, it depends what you need—if you need to be in Paris tomorrow morning to sign a contract, even a coach seat on a jet flight is "better" than all the food, service, and entertaining accommodations on the best luxury liner.[2]

Universities started feeling the economic pressure of cheaper and faster data management, as well as more cost-efficient interactivity, 10

---

[1]James Traub, "Drive-Thru U.: Higher Education for People Who Mean Business," *New Yorker*, October 20 and 27, 1997, 116.

[2]Lew Perelman points out that educational institutions increasingly will be forced to transform themselves in order to meet the various needs of their students, while remaining profitable. See http://www.wcic.org/~wallyrog/hyper2.htm for additional background.

years ago. Library patrons who loved the dusty old stacks and the traditional carrels were surprised in the late 1980s when card catalogs disappeared practically overnight. Dewey Decimal and Library of Congress could exist in harmony in many libraries, but tight budgets couldn't justify $100,000 a year (or more) to keep up a physical display of holdings. The card catalogs were replaced with terminals. Once all the book listings were on-line, it was hard to imagine why students and researchers needed to come to the library anymore to do their search work. It was a small step to make the on-line version of the card catalog available to anyone anywhere. Next it was possible to search the shelves with mouse-clicks at any time of the day or night, instead of roaming the stacks during operating hours. Electronic library exploration offers another advantage as well: the on-line searcher can "see" every volume owned by the library, even those checked out or in use by another patron.

Unbundling Training and Credentialing

The digitizing of the card catalog symbolizes the emancipation of higher education. No longer tied to ivy-covered buildings, the university is now free to unbundle its two primary products: content learning and credentialing. These are two separate functions—learning something and getting a piece of paper that distinguishes you from those who haven't paid tuition and been through the program. This fundamental difference will shape much of the future of training and education.[3] Training will be a salable product; using a growing variety of tools and methodologies, instructors will share facts, knowledge, and insights. At many institutions, the training will be available to anyone who can pay tuition. Credentialing is more complicated; by its very nature, it implies that paying tuition isn't enough. For hundreds of years, students have paid tuition and still *failed* for the simple reason that credentialing implies a standard of performance and the ability to rank individuals by that performance standard. It may begin with stringent application and selection procedures.

Institutions will evolve to meet different needs. Some will concentrate on training, some on credentialing. In every case, success of the 1 to 1 university will depend on the cost-value perceptions of the student-customers.

Visitors to the Stratford Festival in Ontario see top-flight performances of plays by Shakespeare and other playwrights. The Shakespeare

---

[3]Carol A. Twigg, and Diana G. Oblinger, "The Virtual University," a report from a joint EDUCOM/IBM roundtable discussion (Washington, D.C., November 5 and 6, 1996).

pieces are brought to life true to the original language but in costumes and period settings throughout history. Seeing "Julius Caesar" set in 1940s South America, for example, or nineteenth-century costumes for "Much Ado About Nothing," emphasizes the timelessness of the Bard's stories and lines. Some attend the Festival just to be entertained, others go in a deliberate effort to learn and appreciate Shakespeare more. The festival is a way of studying: it's not reading; it's not lecturing; it *is* a greatly enriched learning environment. But it is also a very expensive way to study. Play tickets rival Broadway shows in price, and the captive audience faces expensive accommodation and meal costs for miles around Stratford. It's inefficient—at most, you can study only a handful of Shakespeare's plays in a season. Some students of literature may need a faster or less expensive way to study the Bard (through a college course perhaps, or private study and reading, or seeing films of the plays). The college course offers a credential. Attendance at Stratford plays, no matter how much an individual invests, offers no credential beyond a set of ticket stubs.

The point is that more than one model for universities will prevail. "Traditional" colleges and universities will fade in importance in direct proportion to the dwindling percentage of "traditional" students.

Consider shopping. Today's shopper has an increasing number of alternatives to the original shopping model of a trip to the local store to make selections and haul them home. She can teach Streamline or Net-Grocer her preferences, shop QVC on television or the Sky Mall on an airline phone, shop on-line, or shop in a variety of other ways. Different ways work for different people.

2.3 EMERGING NEW COMPETITORS, SERVING NEW MARKETS OF LEARNERS

Ultimately, what determines which model is best will be defined by which is best for *this* learner at *this* stage in his life. Like more and more organizations across North America and around the world, universities will learn to build one-to-one (1 to 1) Learning Relationships with individual customers (students and learners) as well as the corporate concerns that are already providing much of the funding for tuition and research. Their competition will, increasingly, not be other traditional universities, but will instead be on-line coursework, Web-based learning centers, and corporate centers of learning and education that have expanded beyond their own company's walls. Motorola University began in 1981 as an internal quality training center. By 1990, the program included consulting, and it began providing services to other companies to help them become more efficient and effective within their businesses, with courses ranging from meeting planning to cycle time reduction. Motorola requires each of its employees to complete 40 or more hours a year of job-relevant training through its university. The fastest-growing sector of higher education is, in fact, the "corporate university" that provides training for middle and upper management.[4]

It is important to note that higher education has a variety of different customers. Students, parents, employers, government, states, and donors are just some examples. The most important customer could be the individuals paying the greatest percentage of the bills; the state, for public education; or, for some research institutions, the federal government.

For the purposes of this chapter, students are considered the customers of a college or university. Instead of measuring the success of a university by the number of students enrolled, a 1 to 1 university will gauge its success by the projected increase or decrease in a student's expected future value.

Success for any organization—even universities—will require that 1 to 1 strategies be practiced. The 1 to 1 university will no longer focus just on acquiring more students, but on retaining its existing learners and growing the business each gives the institution.

In the aggregate-market universe—the universe of standardized services, products, and mass marketing—the most widely understood and heavily practiced form of competition is centered on acquisition, not retention, of student and other constituent groups. Of course, the more a competitor focuses on acquiring its rivals' students, faculty, and donors, the more difficult it becomes to keep and grow active and loyal participants. Even target marketing and segmentation strategies are still just mass marketing, only smaller and a bit more sophisticated.

More and more, progressive private and state-funded organizations, like their for-profit models, realize that simply acquiring new customers will not automatically result in success. The Age of Aquarius has become the Age of Interactivity, and success will largely be determined by an organization's ability to manage the relationship with an individual learner—effectively as well as efficiently. This shifts the focus from managing products and services to managing relationships: 1 to 1 universities will anticipate the individual requirements of valued and well-understood learners and corporate partners.

This is not to say that traditional colleges and universities will go away. After all, we went from the Agricultural era to the Industrial era, but we still eat. There just won't be more than 3,000 traditional colleges and universities anymore, just as the majority of the population no

---

[4]Traub at 114–23.

longer farms. As we move from the Industrial Age to the Age of Information and Interactivity, the successful university will be based not on products, but on customers. Success, in the 1 to 1 future, will be defined by a balance between individual participants' needs from the institution and each one's relative value to it.

In the long run, funding will drive the models for education and credentialing. What can learners afford in terms of time and money? How will study and learning fit into the rest of their lives? Is the goal of the educational organization to minimize cost or maximize value (or both, depending on the individual student customer)? What does each participant need from education? Why do they participate in a particular program? The successful organization in the 1 to 1 future will treat different customers differently based on whether a particular individual is looking for a four-year socialization experience, personal enrichment and the satisfaction of curiosity, preparation for the current job she has or the next one she wants, or something else.

What's Driving Organizations to 1 to 1 Strategies Right Now?

Until recently, the computer's impact on business was measured almost exclusively in terms of speed and convenience. Computers first automated routine processes such as accounting, payroll, inventory management, and production. Later, more sophisticated information technology led many businesses to reengineer these work processes altogether, accomplishing tasks in a different order, doing them with fewer personnel, or not doing them at all.

In other words, many organizations and businesses harnessed computers to become more competitive in operations. Universities have already streamlined registration, financial aid, applications, and record keeping, but radically declining information processing costs and rising computational power mandate a radical transformation in the way colleges and universities actually compete for participants.

Product-centered competition has always been based on using research to find the most desired product benefits among a prospective population. By examining a statistical sample of a target population of customers, a firm gleans a scientific picture of the needs and preferences of the majority. Then, after developing products to deliver these benefits, the benefits are advertised to attract potential customers. Some universities started this process as enrollments declined in the 1980s; others adamantly held out for internally determined curriculum models. Many compromised by offering students free choices within groups of coursework to meet basic requirements.

Across all industries, the product-based model for success is now in decline. Instead, computers are already changing a wide variety of firms into genuinely customer-centered, rather than product-centered, organizations. A student-centered, 1 to 1 university would deliver personal, individualized services to each of its thousands, or perhaps millions, of students and learners, based on interaction and feedback from each of these students. It would also remember a complete history for each.

As educational models evolve, institutions of higher education will face not only new competitors but also new opportunities to interact and customize the learning experience for their existing customers. When a university gains new knowledge of an individual student's specifications or needs, two activities are taking place: the university is learning, and the student is teaching. What creates genuine loyalty is the interaction of both these activities. When the reward for the student's effort to teach an enterprise is a more individually satisfactory product or service, the effort makes a student loyal. The students are, through their own efforts, increasing the value of the institutions to *them*.

Treating different customers differently is not a strategy that can simply be grafted onto any university's existing business plan. Instead, it represents a radically different, even daring, orientation for the institution. Some nonprofit organizations, including colleges and universities, are already prospering from embracing 1 to 1 strategies. This chapter focuses on these new competitive rules and how the 1 to 1 university can compete successfully in the Age of Interactivity.

2.4 AGGREGATE MARKETS VERSUS INDIVIDUAL CUSTOMERS

Traditional competition among organizations is based on finding aggregate or group markets of indistinguishable customers (defined during the segmentation process as being identical). But more and more the battleground is shifting to the individual, unique customer. The traditional competitor succeeds by examining a representative sample of potential customers to obtain a scientific picture of their needs and preferences. Once services are developed that deliver these benefits, they are promoted to attract additional potential customers in the same segment.

This aggregate-market competition has been the dominant approach used by nearly every organization, including nonprofits, since the introduction of marketing. In business-to-business situations, the promotion has usually focused on specific, identifiable product features; in consumer marketing, it has often focused on the product's image-oriented, emotional attributes. Relying on increasing computer power to do analyses ever more efficiently, organizations have directed their marketing efforts toward smaller and smaller segments of customers. In the final analysis, though, whether we talk about a mass market or a niche, the aggregate-market competitor treats every individual in each segment the same way, constantly looking for more and more new customers. The best guess on what to do next comes from getting as accurate a fix as possible on their *average* needs.

Beyond improving the aggregate-market competitor's efficiency at finding niches, however, the computer is now changing the actual character of the competitive model itself, supplanting it with a customer-driven model. When we say *customer-driven*, we are talking about a practice that relies on delivering highly tailored, individualized products and services to each customer based on feedback from and interaction with each of these customers. The customer-driven model of competition is based on each organization's specific, individual customer interactions—*one customer at a time.*

2.5 NEW COMPETITIVE RULES

Customer-driven competition is what we call one-to-one (1 to 1) business strategy, a form of marketing that was prohibitively expensive, and therefore nearly inconceivable, to the traditional marketer just a few years ago. Today, as we enter the Age of Interactivity and microchip-controlled products, it has become a prerequisite for competitive success.

Constituent-centered marketing, done 1 to 1 with individual constituents, works because the microchip now makes it possible to integrate the three most important functions of any organization—functions without which no organization can sustain itself: the individual database, interactive dialogue with individual customers, and mass customization of service delivery.

Basically, the new, customer-centered dynamic of the 1 to 1 university works like this:

> *Information:* I know you, individually. You have been my learner before. With my database I can now see how you differ from my other students. I can remember everything about your relationship with me.

> *Communication:* Using new interactive communication vehicles, you give me feedback on how I am doing with you. Then you tell me what works best for you.

> *Production/Service Delivery:* Using mass customization technology, I can now make curriculum or provide a service to your individual

specifications. After I make it, I ask for more feedback: "Was this okay? Want it more this way? All right, how about that?" With every transaction, I get better at giving you exactly what you want.

In essence, computers have now made it possible to create an individual feedback loop, for each customer, integrating the production and service delivery process into the service and communication processes. This feedback loop renders obsolete many traditional marketing principles that organizations used to hold sacred and establishes a totally new dynamic of competition—a dynamic based on competing for one participant at a time.

No longer is the marketer confined to dealing only with awareness levels, or attitudes and brand preferences, or even competitive service comparisons. No longer must he do surveys of potential customers, statistically projecting the results to a larger population. Instead, the participant and the 1 to 1 university together are now redefining what it means to be part of a commercial or nonprofit relationship: I know you. You tell me what makes this work for you. I do it. You tell me if I did it right. I remember. I do it for you again, even better next time.

Because it is now possible to keep precise track of individual relationships with individual members, organizational size alone has become a less potent competitive advantage. That means an organization of any size now has the opportunity to use information about each participant to get more of that individual's participation. It also means that a small organization may be able to beat out a much larger organizations that does not have (or which has but does not use) information about a particular valuable customer. Notwithstanding the "brand" or status value of a handful of high-status Ivy League and top-ranked higher education institutions, getting and keeping more participation will depend primarily on who has and uses the most information about a specific customer, not on who has the most customers. This is one reason share of customer will replace market share as the most important measure of success in the 1 to 1 future.

2.6   THE ONE-TO-ONE ENTERPRISE

Adopting the 1 to 1 model is not as straightforward as identifying an additional niche market, for now the marketing process itself can no longer be confined to recruitment, public relations, or the ad agency. One-to-one marketing, because it requires an integrative approach to dealing with customers individually, cannot simply be strapped on to an organization's other marketing efforts. To compete in a truly customer-driven way, the 1 to 1 university must integrate its entire range of business functions around satisfying the individual needs of each individual member—not just marketing, customer service, and sales and channel management, but service delivery, logistics, and financial measurement and metrics. To ensure the efficient integration of these functions around individual members, the enterprise's organizational structure itself must in many cases also be altered. The organization must embrace significant change, affecting virtually every department, division, administrator, and employee, every product, every service, and every function.

However, the reward for becoming a 1 to 1 university is immense. The 1 to 1 university will be able to generate unprecedented levels of participant loyalty by offering an unprecedented level of customization and relationship-building. The result at both large and small organizations (including 3M, Hewlett-Packard, Pitney Bowes, and a number of others) has been spectacularly profitable.

Specifying and Remembering

The reason customization is such a powerful competitive strategy is partly—but only partly—due to the member's increased satisfaction with a better tailored product. The organization will not necessarily realize a sustainable advantage just from the fact that a member can get a service (or communication, or motivation) tailored perfectly to his own needs. That is, once the technology is adopted by everyone and a number of other organizations offer customization, then a member will be able to get satisfaction anywhere, so tailoring or increased services do not of themselves provide a long-term competitive advantage. What gives customization its real strength is that it allows an organization to make itself practically invulnerable to competition from other organizations, even when those other organizations eventually do the same thing in the same way.

The secret to keeping and growing a single customer forever is participation, which can also be thought of as collaboration. It's the effort on the part of the customer that results in a better product or service than he can get anywhere else from anyone who isn't so far up his learning curve. The organization that learns from every interaction with a participant will be able to tailor each successive interaction better: It will know how often to contact that individual, and when; it will learn which media to use, or never use, to communicate with a participant; and it will understand the particular interests and motivations that inspire desirable activity in this particular individual. At this point, before any customer can get an equivalent level of service from a computer—even one that offers the same level of interaction and customization—the customer must start all over, and first teach this new organization what he has already taught the original one. The resulting association between an organization and its constituents is a *1 to 1 Learning Relationship.*

How a Learning Relationship Works

A Learning Relationship ensures that it is always in the customer's self-interest to remain with the organization with which he or she first developed the relationship. This goes beyond emotional attachment, and beyond a customer's favoritism for any organization, which may or may not be derived from some sense of obligation or duty. Instead, by establishing a Learning Relationship, the 1 to 1 enterprise increases customer retention simply by making loyalty more rewarding for the customer than nonloyalty. It works this way:

1. The customer tells the enterprise what she wants, through interaction and feedback.

2. The enterprise meets these specifications by customizing its product or service or communications to the needs of that particular customer; then it remembers these specifications.

3. Over time, with more interaction and feedback, the customer will have spent time and energy teaching the enterprise about her own individual needs. The customer will have added value to the relationship.

4. Now, to get an equivalent level of service and reward from any other organization, even one offering the same level of customization and feedback, this customer would first have to reteach the competitor what she has already taught the original enterprise.

2.7   COMPETING IN THE CUSTOMER DIMENSION

One useful method for contrasting the objectives and tactics of a 1 to 1 enterprise with traditional business strategies is to visualize competing for business in a different dimension. The aggregate-market competitor operates in the *product* dimension, whereas the customer-driven, 1 to 1 university enterprise competes in the *customer* dimension. To be successful, any organization must accomplish two basic tasks:

1. It must satisfy some need.

2. It must find someone who wants that need satisfied.

Satisfying customer needs is the quintessential definition of any organization's ultimate reason for being. As Peter Drucker says, everything else—production, engineering, logistics, accounting—everything other than satisfying a customer's need, is just cost.[5]

If we were to map these two tasks—satisfying needs and reaching customers—on a simple two-dimensional graph, the traditional organization would visualize its task as in Exhibit 2–1.

The organization driven by an aggregate-market approach focuses on one product or service at a time, satisfying one basic customer need. Then the organization plumbs the market to find as many customers as possible who want that need satisfied in the current selling period. Aggregate-market competition is inherently product-centered, whether that "product" is a baccalaureate degree, or a one-day seminar, or the intangible college experience.

There is, however, an entirely different way to view the competitive task—a customer-driven approach. Instead of focusing on one need at a time and trying to find as many customers as possible who want that need satisfied, the customer-driven competitor—the 1 to 1 enterprise—focuses on one customer at a time and tries to satisfy as many of that particular customer's needs as possible. To the 1 to 1 university, the marketing battle is fought not in a product dimension but in a customer dimension (see Exhibit 2–2).

A lot can be understood about the difference between traditional, market-driven competition and 1 to 1, customer-driven competition by comparing these two illustrations. The direction of success for an aggregate-market organization is to acquire more customers (that is, to widen the horizontal bar), whereas the direction of success for the customer-driven organization is to keep customers longer and grow them bigger. The width of the horizontal bar can be thought of as a firm's market share: the proportion of members who have their need satisfied by the organization. But the 1 to 1 enterprise focuses on share of customer, represented by the height of the vertical bar.

The aggregate-market organization competes by differentiating products, whereas the 1 to 1 enterprise competes by differentiating customers. The traditional, aggregate marketer tries to establish either an actual product differentiation (with new products and product extensions) or a perceived one (with advertising). The 1 to 1 university, cater-

---

[5]Peter F. Drucker (U.S. writer, educator, management consultant) says, "Business has only two basic functions—marketing and innovation. Everything else is just cost." *The Practice of Management: A Study of the Most Important Function in American Society* (Harperbusiness, 1993).

Exhibit 2–1
AGGREGATE-MARKET COMPETITION

ing to one customer at a time, relies on differentiating each customer from all the others.

These two kinds of competition do not conflict with each other. That is, the horizontal and vertical bars are not opposites, they are orthogonal. This means, first, that the strategies and tactics appropriate to one kind of competition are simply not relevant, and thus not easily applied, to the other. Second, it means that the 1 to 1 enterprise can, in fact, pursue both types of strategies simultaneously. In other words, there is no reason every 1 to 1 enterprise should not be concerned just as much with getting customers as it is with keeping them and growing them.

In the traditional, aggregate-market business model, interaction with individual members is not necessary, and feedback from particular members is useful only insofar as it is representative of the market as a whole. An aggregate-market competitor produces and delivers the same product, meeting a single need, in basically the same way for everyone in any given market. In contrast, the 1 to 1 university must interact with each participant over time, using the customer's feedback from this interaction to deliver a customized product or service. It is a time-dependent, evolutionary process. The product, communication, or service is increasingly tailored and the customer is more and more precisely differentiated from other individuals.

In contrast to the traditional marketer, the 1 to 1 enterprise takes advantage of advancing technologies in information and interactivity to

Exhibit 2–2
CUSTOMER-DRIVEN COMPETITION

get as great a share of each constituent's participation as possible. The 1 to 1 organization knows that different customers return different levels of payback. Understanding how customers compare in terms of their expected contributions to an organization is critical for success.

The two most useful differences among participants—differences that define the strategy for the 1 to 1 enterprise—are *needs* and *valuations.* Customers have different needs from an organization, and they represent different values to an organization. All other types of participant description—demographics, psychographics, firmographics, employment record, life experience, geographic origin, satisfaction level, Scholastic Achievement Test scores or grade point average, extracurriculars—are just proxies for discovering the student's needs and value.

2.8 CUSTOMER VALUATION

The traditional, aggregate-market competitor treats all customers essentially the same way. This is true for nonprofit organizations that make rough cuts by donation size. Benefactors' names may be bigger on the commemorative plaque than those of Friends; Platinum donors may get handwritten thank-yous as opposed to the preprinted notes of appreciation sent to Bronze-level donors. But all the Platinum donors get the same handwritten message, and Benefactors all appear on the plaque in the same typeface. They all receive the same benefits, they are charged the same price, and they get basically the same message. At universities, honor students, or secondary education majors, or freshmen, or executive education students may get an offering different from those for other students, but within each group each student will get the same basic offering. If, however, we acknowledge that each student is unique, then we can take full advantage of the fact that some customers are simply more valuable than others, even within categories.

To think about member valuation the right way, we need to use two concepts: the member's *actual*, current valuation and the member's *strategic* or potential valuation.

The ideal expression of actual valuation is customer lifetime value (LTV), that is, the stream of expected future value, net of costs, of a student's monetary and other contributions, discounted at some appropriate rate back to its net present value. Note that the contributions from a student's relationship with an institution are not necessarily derived just from future monetary revenues. Students may also give an institution other benefits, such as referrals of other students, volunteer time and efforts, willingness to be recognized as alumni, successful-alumni status, and help in improving the organization's offerings, among other things.

From this stream of contributions we must then deduct expenses. Maintaining any sort of relationship over time will require communicating individually (via phone, fax, Web, mail, e-mail, personal contact, and so forth), as well as setting up information systems necessary to track and remember interactions. These costs must not only be calculated but, whenever possible, also allocated to the specific individuals to whom they apply. The purpose here is to compare a university's constituents, and we will be able to compare them more and more accurately as information technology makes increasingly sophisticated modeling possible.

In the Interactive Age, as more organizations learn how to treat different customers differently, the value of a particular customer determines the level of administrative time and investment that can be allocated to that customer, either to make the customer more loyal or to gain a greater share of that customer's participation. Some will flinch at the implications of apparent economic discrimination here. But consider: The excellent students and the poorest students have always required the most time and energy from good professors, and the extra attention pays off more for these extremes than for the average student. Likewise, the student who will participate actively in lifelong learning, who will recommend seminars and courses to colleagues, and who will participate in developmental or research programs justifies more frequent communication and interaction, and therefore a higher level of expenditure, than the infrequent or even average participant.

Student-customer valuation will require measures of success based on individual student results, not just product or program measures. Rather than seeing whether a particular course enrolled enough students to justify its existence, for example, the institution will also see whether a particular student is valuable enough to justify a certain level of expenditure. Some commercial organizations are already beginning to think in terms of "customer equity," and asking themselves whether it would be acceptable for a product to be unprofitable so long as every customer is profitable. This will be an uncomfortable question for most traditional institutions to acknowledge at first. But it is the first step to setting up a model—or in the short run, a set of proxy variables—for calculating current lifetime value (LTV) as well as strategic (or potential) valuation by participant. The 1 to 1 institution will be able to calculate share of customer on an individual, participant-by-participant basis, with the goal of capturing a greater share of dollars, time, and other investment in learning. (This may mean that competitors are not only other degree-granting institutions, but include software retailers and the Discovery Channel.)

Mass Customizing to Meet Individual Student Needs

Differentiating student-customers by their long-term value is one of the two important ways to differentiate them. Understanding and predicting *each* student-customer's needs, however, represents the strategic key to continued and additional contributions from that individual. The 1 to 1 enterprise understands and is able to satisfy different students' various motivational and interactivity needs, in addition to learning and credentialing.

It is not, therefore, possible to discuss long-term Learning Relationships without discussing mass customization. A growing number of commercial organizations are not only learning how to mass customize but why: because each interaction with a customer makes the company more valuable to the customer, who won't want to start over with another company that can't act on what the customer has taught the original company. Dell mass customizes computers. Saturn makes cars to order. Shoes and blue jeans are mass customized to fit perfectly. One credit card company offers a credit card in 11,000 different configurations. Many for-profit companies are learning that technology has altered the old rule of economies of scale and have discovered that make-to-order can actually be *less* costly than standardization.

The 1 to 1 university will build a Learning Relationship with each participant by interacting over time, and continuing to increase its level of relevance to each student-customer by understanding motivation, price-value, and need for convenience for each student-customer. What are the motivations behind this participation? Although participation in a center of higher learning should be motivation enough, the 1 to 1 university will understand whether this student, for example, is taking a course because of interest in material, admiration for the professor, a need to be respected, a desire to make business contacts, as part of a degree program, career preparation, or some other reason that makes participation in this course rewarding. Remembering what each participant wants and finding ways to make the collaboration effort valuable to the participant leads to mass customizing the offer, the response, the dialogue process, frequency, channel, the level of recognition, the opportunity for active participation, and so on.

Understanding How People Learn

Some people will always find that a lecture environment works best for them. Others will prefer group settings, and still others might only want an occasional concentrated day of learning. Some want only the learning, and others value the credential as well. The point is, whatever learning techniques or "1 to 1 university" design people prefer, institutions will have to begin mass customizing the education process in order to separate how people want to learn in an Interactive Age, and how people earn credentials/degrees.

International Learning Systems (http://www.ILSInc.com) in Golden, Colorado, specializes in executive training and professional development. In some cases, ILS recommends that a client first examine how its employees learn, one employee at a time, before working together to train individuals. To help people learn more effectively, ILS begins by identifying how each individual best works within the organization. For example, some people learn and retain information more easily in small group classes, whereas others benefit more from intensive hands-on applications.

ILS has designed four distinct learning categories[6] to cluster individuals:

1. Self-study—where individuals learn best by reading or through hands-on experiences

[6]This study, conducted by ILS, reported that among the four clusters, there was no significant difference based on an individual's position, job title, work environment, responsibilities, shift, job location, or hours worked. *The ILS Report* (a quarterly publication) in Spring 1995 summarized the results of this research.

2. Watch and listen—where videotapes or audiotapes speed learning

3. Partner—where lessons and question-and-answer sessions with only an instructor are the most helpful

4. Group—where a lecture format is the easiest way to learn

One client ILS helped (an engineering firm) began by assigning each individual employee into one of these four groups. At the beginning of the training, the engineers were at 23 percent proficiency. After five and a half weeks, all employees soared to 100 percent proficiency. Within the CAD industry, this intensive training typically would have taken eight months.

Creating an Ongoing Dialogue with Student-Customers

The simple truth is that the more dialogue a firm has with a customer, the more opportunity exists to get an accurate picture of strategic value (the potential future value), as well as the opportunity for mass customization. Any good salesperson knows that one of the most important pieces of information for a sales database is a customer's estimate of future buying needs and information on what competitors the customer is dealing with at present.

The 1 to 1 organization determines each customer's Preferred Media Package (PMP) and communicates with each individual using the media channels most comfortable for each. The 1 to 1 organization learns to monitor the effectiveness, not just the cost-efficiency, of dialogue interactions. (We have a friend who is ready to give up on a local charity. She is happy to send them $35 a year, but that's all. Yet they mail her a request for a contribution every three to four weeks. She hates knowing that most of the money she contributes will become junk mail sent back to her in the form of futile attempts to inspire more frequent contributions.)

Every communication with a member and every response from a customer has the potential to tell a 1 to 1 enterprise more about exactly what that particular customer wants. If a firm is not often in direct touch with its customers, then every tiny contact is a priceless opportunity to learn more and act accordingly.

Having a dialogue with your customers does not consist of doing a series of 1 to 1 interviews with actual customers in order to get feedback for the marketing plan. That kind of sample-and-projection research is important (even critical) to any successful marketing effort, but it is only dialogue with the particular customers involved in the research effort. It is only a sample.

Having a dialogue does not consist of sending out millions of pieces of mail and making a sale to 0.5 percent of the addressees. It is not dialogue if you make sales to 2 percent, or even 10 percent, of the addressees. Most mass mailings are simply monologues in an addressable format. They are little more than broadcast soliloquies, with envelopes and stamps. Many organizations do it with their current customers as well as prospects, but it is not dialogue.

Conducting a dialogue with a customer is, in a sense, having an exchange of thoughts. It is a form of mental collaboration. It may include handling a participant inquiry, but it should not be limited to that. It could mean gathering background information on the participant, but it should not be limited to that, either.

In the face of rising consumer cynicism, time pressure, and impatience, a dialogue marketer will remain a dependable collaborator with his participants. Instead of the sales-oriented commercials and advertisements that characterize much of today's mass-media barrage, tomorrow's successful share-of-member marketer will be inviting a consumer to begin and sustain a dialogue.

2.9   CAN 1 TO 1 APPLY TO NONPROFITS?

Beyond creating an interactive dialogue with individual students, nonprofit organizations should also focus on implementing 1 to 1 strategies among their base of donor-customers. Private, public, and nonprofit organizations alike are worried about staying in front of the technological tidal wave that is making products smarter and empowering customers to *expect* customized services. As more and more nonprofits learn how to target their donor markets, individuals with the ability and willingness to donate are increasingly bombarded. Everyone finds them, everyone mails to them, and everyone calls them. Philanthropic organizations today, more than ever before, are searching for strategies that will enable them to cement donor loyalty and get a greater share of each donor's charitable dollar or volunteer time. Many are already experiencing success with individualized, 1 to 1 strategies.

A growing number of postsecondary training and credentialing programs will run for profit and will balance curriculum considerations with profitability issues, based on customer equity. Many other organizations will maintain their privately or publicly supported nonprofit status. The 1 to 1 approach has been used successfully for fund-raising at more than one nonprofit organization. Ken Burnett, chairman of Burnett Associates in London, reports several cases of successful 1 to 1 applications by nonprofit organizations.[7]

Should You Let Your Supporters Refuse Your Mailings?

Botton Village is a small rural working community for mentally handicapped adults. Since it started fund-raising in 1983, it has been committed to the donor-based approach.

As soon as it was able, it decided to offer its supporters choices: the choice of how often they wished to hear from the Village, the choice of what they wanted to hear about, and the choice of whether they wanted to receive appeals. Most radically, it offered current donors who receive four or five appeals each year the chance to get just one appeal, at Christmas time. Or, if they wished, they could opt out of receiving appeals altogether and just get the Village newspaper on its own.

The response to this strange approach has been outstanding. Around 11,000 of Botton's 50,000 donors have so far opted to receive just one appeal each year, and a further 1,200 have asked for the newspaper only. Many said they wished all other charities could be so considerate and thoughtful.

But the most spectacular aspect is that over the last three years, Botton's "Christmas Only" segment has responded at around 50 percent (once reaching 56 percent)—substantially more and at less cost than the Village would have incurred if it had sent all the regular mailings to every contributor throughout the year. Even more impressively, the "newsletter only" segment, which does not even get a reply form, nevertheless brings in around 9 percent each issue in spontaneous response; at Christmas, this rate shoots up above 25 percent. During this time, gift averages have also consistently been exceptionally high. By communicating with each member as that particular member wants, Botton generates higher donations, at substantially lower cost, and is able with less effort to spend more of each donation on its actual charity work and less on raising funds.

Does It Make Sense to Offer Your Donors Their Money Back?

Greenpeace is one of the world's best known groups. As an organization with a strong corporate culture, it is also naturally in tune with the donor-based approach, even if it has not always practiced it. Recently,

[7]Ken Burnett, *Relationship Fundraising: A Donor-Based Approach to the Business of Raising Money* (London: White Lion Press Limited, 1992).

Greenpeace UK successfully raised a large sum of money from its supporters to pay anticipated court costs of $400,000.

The judge in this court case did rule against Greenpeace, but as a gesture of support for their ideals, he did not award costs to the adversary, British Nuclear Fuels. Greenpeace could have kept quiet about this, but instead it wrote back to each supporter offering to give his or her money back. Only six people took the refund! The rest gladly told Greenpeace to keep it. Some sent a further gift. Stronger ties were formed, simply as a result of Greenpeace's honesty with each donor.

Will It Help to Let Your Donors Share Their Feelings?

Britain's National Trust is one of the world's largest membership organizations, but until recently many National Trust people believed that the primary reason members joined was to get discounts on entry to the Trust's sites of national heritage. Now they are not sure.

When launching its committed giving strategy, called Centenary Guardians, the National Trust included a simple card on which it invited respondents to submit their favorite anecdote of a visit to a National Trust property. The completed return cards they received were not only far more numerous than anticipated, but came from all ages and contained insights into the motivations and emotions of their supporters, which were even more welcome and unexpected.

Donors sent treasured photographs and moving poems; they also talked with grateful enthusiasm about favorite places of childhood memory or of where they had accepted a proposal of marriage. Many used the cards as a way of saying something they had perhaps wanted to say for ages. One man even used it to inform the Trust of a substantial legacy!

The appeal, by the way, was a resounding success, due in no small measure to the happy feelings it evoked instead of being just another request for funds. And it really motivated the National Trust staff.

2.10   COLLEGES AND UNIVERSITIES ARE ALREADY DOING IT

Technology is changing the world. Interactivity is affecting everything from grocery shopping to in-flight service on airplanes to the way people learn. The implications for higher education are immense. How does interactivity affect postsecondary education? What lessons can we learn from the pioneers?

Western Governor's University is creating independent and objective measurements of "output"—their graduates. Rather than measuring the university's quality by the number of Ph.D.s on the faculty or books in the library, the institution will rate the academic performance

of its students against an objective measure of the student's overall ac-
complishment (not just a GPA, which is itself merely an accumulation
of micromeasurements). Governor Roy Romer of Colorado calls it
"competency verification."[8] When recruiters or corporations want to interview students, WGU will identify students who best meet the inter-
viewer's needs.

Franklin University in Columbus, Ohio, assigns a Student Service
Associate (SSA) to each student at the application stage. That SSA serves
as the student's "customer manager" throughout the student's experience at Franklin, the one person to call with any issue or problem. The
Student Union was designed for the nontraditional student. Instead of a
place to hang out and kill time, the Union is set up so the busy adult student can get administrative errands done quickly and efficiently. President Paul Otte's goal is to free up as much time as possible for student
learning by reducing the amount of student time spent on administrivia.

**Duke University's GEMBA and WEMBA at the Fuqua School of
Business** both use distance learning to bring the opportunity of MBA
study to a growing number of students who cannot participate in the
traditional full-time, five-day-a-week program. The Weekend Executive
MBA (WEMBA) program follows the traditional daytime curriculum,
but meets on Friday and Saturday. The Global Executive MBA (GEMBA)
program is Internet-based, meets occasionally in one of five cities
worldwide, takes 19 months to complete, and costs $82,000.

University of Phoenix students are often underwhelmed at its physical facilities—a suite of offices where 40,000 students (up from 3,000 a
decade ago) are managed. But they are glad to participate in U.P.'s accredited baccalaureate programs in business, nursing, and education, as well
as an MBA program—and to get the education on their terms, in their
schedules. Only one-sixth of America's college enrollees fit the stereotype
of full-time students living on campus; U.P.'s students want "the kind of
relationship they had with their bank," according to Arthur Levine, president of Teachers College at Columbia University, quoted in an article
about U.P.[9] The University of Phoenix is one of the few institutions where
you can get an entire degree without ever physically meeting your professor or fellow students. This means that U.P.'s market is literally global.

Westcott Executive Education Network links Westcott Communications Inc., the Wharton School, and eight other business schools to

---

[8]For a complete discussion of alternative measurements developed by
Western Governors University, see the interview with Roy Romer, "A
Matter of Degrees," *Educom Review* 32 (January/February 1997). See
http://www.educom.edu/web/pubs/review/reviewArticles/32116.html for the
entire interview.

[9]Traub at 116.

provide executive programs, live, by satellite. Executives at companies such as Hewlett-Packard, Johnson & Johnson, EDS, Eastman Kodak, Texas Instruments, and others can interact (using two-way audio and keypads) with a cross-section of peers, as well as faculty.

2.11   WHAT WOULD IT BE LIKE TO BE A STUDENT AT A 1 TO 1 UNIVERSITY?

There would be no lines for registration, financial aid, or the bursar's office! Well, almost no lines would exist. The e-business unit at IBM and the University of Minnesota (UM) partnered to leverage existing legacy systems to deliver Web-based solutions for students.

Some of the various services available at all four UM campuses include:

- On-line registration. Nearly 300 students can simultaneously log in and register for classes; the system is available both on and off campus.

- Personal course planner. Remember the days of scheduling an appointment with faculty members for advising? UM has made it possible for students to research courses on-line and to receive alerts to scheduling conflicts.

- Financial aid estimator. Information about applications and eligibility is available for scholarships, grants, and loans. Data from the bursar about tuition and fees is used to help accurately reflect an individual student's situation.

- Web calendar. Students can plot their course of study to determine what classes must be completed—and when—if they are to graduate by their target date. E-mail notification is even available for students to receive reminders about fast-approaching deadlines.

- Customized enrollment statement. Some of the information summarized in one statement includes: course information and the faculty teaching each class, fees and tuition bills, required textbooks, final exam schedules, and course drop/add deadlines.

The university invested $500,000 over a period of 2 years and expects to save nearly half of its investment ($200,000) *each year* in administrative costs alone. Registration staff already has been reduced by 20 percent.

IBM plans to customize this tool for other universities and colleges. Imagine other extensions:

- Each student has a personal advisor, available via the Web.
- Click here to renew your Pell grant. Application due Friday.
- You will register on-line for spring semester between Thursday at 8 A.M. and Friday at midnight. Click here to review your course credits and requirements for graduation.
- Your next installment invoice will be printed Tuesday. Click here if you prefer to have it e-mailed—to yourself or your parents—and save the $10 paperwork fee.
- Get a free orange juice tomorrow at breakfast by answering these three questions about our meal service.
- Because you usually attend all the musical performances, we wanted to remind you that the Brass Quintet will be here next week, and you haven't bought tickets yet.
- Your History 360 prof just found an article you need to read before Wednesday's class. Click here to download the text.

The 1 to 1 nonresident student would get similar reminders, plus notification of relevant course and seminar opportunities. The institution would use community knowledge to predict what this student-customer is most likely to need next by comparing this learner's reactions to others who have rated the same courses and experiences the same way.

The 1 to 1 corporate learning center will understand what skills departments and divisions need, and deliver the learning for those skills to the right people, on a just-in-time basis, often using nontraditional methodologies.[10]

The 1 to 1 alum would get information about the local alumni chapter wherever she lives. She could get an individually printed alum newsletter magazine that emphasizes her personal professors, sorority news, cohort group, etc. She may participate in Reunions-by-Web or chat rooms by class.

The 1 to 1 learning institution will not broadcast information about itself and its offerings and expect students to get the information and take the initiative. Instead, the 1 to 1 learning institution will get information about students and take the initiative on the student's behalf: "Here's the next thing you need us to do for you, and here are some ways to get it that may work best for you."

---

[10]For a specific discussion of learning with multimedia tools, see Lew Perelman's comments at http://www.wcic.org/~wallyrog/hyper1.htm.

There's no doubt that the university of the future will require some out-of-the-box thinking, and a major revision in culture and organization. Five thousand years ago, priests emerged as specialists in the creation and dissemination of information.[11] Collectively, they formed the repositories of knowledge—something like human libraries. Writing and recording emerged for two reasons: for basic bookkeeping and accounting in the marketplace, and to make the oral tradition of the priest-libraries more durable. Libraries shifted to buildings housing books. Scholars came to the books and students came to the scholars. It's possible that academic departments were formed based on classification of library volumes. This form of university study has endured more or less intact for 2,500 years. Now digital technology renders unnecessary the physical proximity of scholars to their universities, or to their students, for that matter.

The cost of the physical university increases exponentially. Real estate under ivy-covered buildings is often far more valuable than the buildings themselves. Tenured professors cost more to maintain than part-time instructors. A subscription to *Chemical Abstracts* cost $12/year in 1940, $3,500/year in 1977, and $17,400/year today.[12] As this cost rises, the role of the university shifts from physical repository of knowledge to electronic access to knowledge. The professor is liberated; departments (and perhaps programs and degrees) may form around physically separated groups of scholars who themselves may no longer work as university employees but as freelance, independent speakers and researchers.

2.12 CONCLUSION

Although it sounds new, and today it depends on information technology, the truth is that interactive, 1 to 1 marketing has been around as long as civilization. Before the Industrial Revolution, a merchant or craftsman remembered each of his customers individually. His customers would tell him what they wanted, and then the craftsman would make it for them. This approach utilized interactivity, customization, and database marketing, but the craftsman carried the database in his own head. This model applied not just to crafted products, but to services and every other type of commercial enterprise as well.

Toyama no KusuriUri is a way of doing business in Japan. This business approach, used primarily by medical supply companies, works on an automatic replenishment basis. A customer receives a medicine cabinet filled with different medicines that might be useful for a variety of sicknesses. Periodically a salesperson stops by, opens the medicine

---

[11]Eli M. Noam, "Electronics and the Dim Future of the University," *Science* 270 (13 October 1995): 247.

[12]*Id.*

cabinet, and charges the customer for whatever supplies have been used since the last visit, similar to the way a hotel room mini-bar works.

The salesperson is careful to write down the medicines that each household consumes, entering this information by hand into the Toyama no KusuriUri customer database, called *Daifuku cho*. Based on the medicines a household has used, the salesperson may make recommendations for other kinds of cures and medicines used by other households with similar consumption patterns.

Toyama no KusuriUri began as a way of business in 1750. The fact that this strategy is still being practiced with the descendants of many of the families originally acquired as customers nearly 250 years ago demonstrates the tremendous competitive power of 1 to 1 marketing. The products inside the cabinets have changed, but the customers remain the same.

For every organization offering postsecondary education, the courses will change with increasing velocity. The politics will shift and the professors will come and go. Over a lifetime, however, it's the customer-student who may remain the same. The student will stay with the organization that remembers how she learns best and predicts the next logical thing she will need in a price-format combination, with or without credentialing.

Remember that there will always be more to do and further to go in this transition. However, just because a complete transition is impossible does not mean it is not useful to start. Technology developments are driving the 1 to 1 strategy in businesses and nonprofit organizations. Since the velocity of technological change is accelerating, the ability of an enterprise to optimize its use of the technology will always be in flux—a process, rather than an endpoint. There are some understandable, practical, and effective strategies for pushing your organization in the 1 to 1 direction: knowing who your participants are and remembering what they tell you; trying to manage your organization's behavior to treat different participants differently; delivering what each individual wants; and creating more ways to receive feedback from student-customers, as cost-efficiently as possible.

Put a few of these strategies together and pretty soon you will see positive results in the strength of your organization's competitive situation. You will be playing by different rules and competing in a different dimension. Be the first 1 to 1 organization on your block and take over your learning and credentialing arena. Treat different participants differently—then keep them, forever.

Today, as information technology allows organizations to remember their customers individually, interact with them, and customize products, services, and information to their individual specifications, every successful organization will return to highly personalized, one-to-one marketing.

CHAPTER THREE

The Revolution in Health Care and a Prognosis for Higher Education*

THOMAS R. DONNELLY, JR.

Senior Vice President of
The Jefferson Group
Formerly Assistant Secretary for Legislation for the
Department of Health and Human Services

JERRY MACARTHUR HULTIN**

Undersecretary of the Navy
Formerly Vice Chairman, Jefferson Partners

STUART H. RAKOFF, PH.D.

Vice President
The Jefferson Group

*The authors would like to thank Andrew Lachman, Rebecca Wind, Katherine Myers, and Kimberly Firetag for their valuable assistance in preparing this chapter.

**The views presented here are those of Jerry MacArthur Hultin and do not necessarily represent the views of the Department of Defense, any of its components, or the Department of the Navy.

3.1   INTRODUCTION

The impact of new market and technological forces on major industries and institutions during the past 20 years has created revolutionary change in both the American and global economies. The banking, automotive, steel, real estate, and health care industries, for example, have each undergone substantial stress and shifts, yet higher education, though not unchanged, has fended off these forces to a large degree. To better understand these forces of change and their likely impact on higher education, we have taken a look at an analogous but not identical industry—health care—in search of illumination and insights.

Health care and higher education have much in common. Both produce products that are largely intangible, highly valued, and difficult to measure. Both are dominated by providers for whom traditional market pressures have been secondary to professional considerations. Traditional institutions in both environments find their previous dominance now challenged by emerging organizational forms. In both, the role of government as provider, funder, and standard-setter has changed dramatically in recent years. Also, in both medicine and higher education, advances in technology (especially information technologies) offer substantial opportunities, and pose substantial risks, for product improvement and system efficiency and effectiveness.

In this chapter, we explore some of the most important dimensions of the ongoing revolution in health care that have changed the nature of this major industry. Although we do not expect that changes and characteristics of the health care system will be completely congruent with those of higher education, there are, we believe, substantial lessons for higher education to be learned from considering how market forces and actors in the health care arena have shaped the emergence of new provider, institutional, consumer, and government behavior, relationships, and expectations.

The first section of this chapter describes the major characteristics of the changing health care market and begins to draw parallels to higher education. In § 3.3, these characteristics are explored in more depth along six primary dimensions: professional providers, institutions, consumers, payers, technology, and systems. Section 3.4 highlights the drivers of change in health care markets and organization, again pointing to the similarities with higher education; § 3.5 draws these parallels even finer by focusing on the changes now occurring in higher education. Finally, § 3.6 offers a prognosis of how the experience of health care may continue to play out for higher education.

3.2   HEALTH CARE AND HIGHER EDUCATION: AN OVERVIEW

The provision of health care services may well be the largest single segment of the U.S. economy. With total annual expenditures exceeding $1 trillion, accounting for almost 14 percent of total gross domestic product (GDP), and employing 9.75 million workers, the health care business touches every American. A complex and fluid set of relationships among consumers, professional and institutional providers, payers, government regulators and policy makers, and technology has created an environment in which many of the major characteristics of the health care system have undergone substantial change in the past thirty years.

Our review of these defining characteristics and changes is intended to raise questions and possible parallels to the complex relationships and changes in the higher education arena. For that purpose, we focus here on but a few major elements of the total health care market and system.

The Product Is Elusive

We often measure and assess health care products by the absence of sickness, rather than through a more positive measure of well-being. And, of course, the very nature of the concept of health is both highly individualized and value-laden. Is it any wonder, then, that the health care system has had so much difficulty measuring its outputs or outcomes? Education is also difficult to define and measure, and hence to assess. How much is too much? How can resources be divided or tradeoffs made? These issues increasingly vex health care managers, policy makers, and consumers, and are beginning to concern higher education managers as well.

A corollary concern is understanding the quality of the product that is produced by the health care system. The health care debate has begun to shift its focus from cost of care to the quality of the care being provided, especially in terms of appropriateness and effectiveness. There is substantial evidence that despite health care expenditures that are substantially higher than any other nation and access to unmatched sophistication in high-intensity medicine, Americans have poorer average outcomes on many measures of health status. Recent reviews have found that Americans use intensive care units five to ten times more than patients in other industrialized countries, with at least questionable comparative outcomes.[1] Others have noted great variations in the use of therapeutic and diagnostic procedures in different regions, again with no measurable evidence of better outcomes. Like health care, despite huge investments, there is also growing evidence that higher education in the United States is falling behind other nations in the effectiveness of learning activities, as reflected in test scores and slow adoption of new technologies that can extend the opportunities of higher education to an even wider population.[2]

The Costs of Health Care Have Exploded

In 1960, total national expenditures for health care services totaled $26.9 billion. By 1995, the total health care bill had climbed to almost $1 trillion. As shown in Exhibits 3–1 and 3–2, the per capita cost of health care climbed from $726 to $3,621 (in constant 1995 dollars), and the percentage of the gross domestic product (GDP) devoted to health care almost tripled, from 5.1 percent to 13.6 percent. Costs of higher education have experienced similar startling increases in recent years, exceeding inflation and raising the cost of traditional institutions beyond the means of many families. The cost of sending one child to a private university has increased from 20 percent to 40 percent of median family income in the past 15 years.[3]

Sources of Funds for Health Care Have Also Shifted

In 1960, 75 percent of health care spending originated in the private sector—primarily consumers and employers. By 1995, that fraction had

[1]W.A. Knaus, "International Comparisons of Intensive Care," *Intensive Care Medicine* 22 (1995): 156-57.

[2]Sir John Daniel, Vice-Chancellor of Britain's Open University, made this point in his keynote address to the 1997 Annual Conference of the American Association for Higher Education, and in his book *Mega-universities and Knowledge Media: Technology Strategies for Higher Education* (London: Kogan Page, 1996).

[3]Daniel, *op. cit.*

Exhibit 3–1
CHANGES IN NATIONAL HEALTH CARE COST PER CAPITA
(1995 DOLLARS)

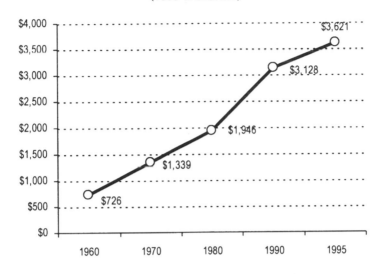

Exhibit 3–2
PERCENTAGE CHANGES IN NATIONAL HEALTH CARE
COSTS AS PERCENTAGE OF GDP

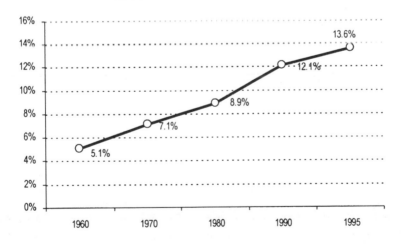

declined to 54 percent. The difference has been filled by significantly greater government participation. The federal government share has increased from 11 percent of total spending in 1960 to 33 percent in 1995. Exhibit 3–3 is a graphic presentation of these trends. In higher education, a shift is also under way, as traditional research funding sources decline, state governments reduce their support of higher education,

Exhibit 3–3
PERCENTAGE CHANGES IN SOURCES OF NATIONAL HEALTH EXPENDITURES

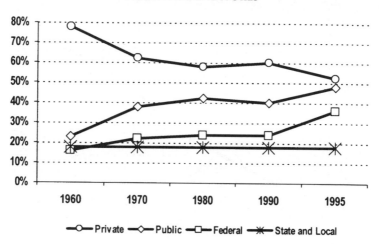

tuition increases begin to slow, and more of the burden falls to increased federal funding, especially for broader student loan programs.

One defining characteristic of the health care market is that the consumers of care often do not pay for that care themselves, at least directly, at the point and time of service. Health insurance is a customary benefit of employment in the United States. Most nonworkers have health insurance coverage through one of the major government programs, Medicare or Medicaid. The same phenomenon is also true in higher education, where parents (and increasingly employers and financial institutions) are paying for the education that students receive.

Participant Roles Have Changed Substantially

Individual professional providers of services in the health care arena, primarily physicians, have gone from being largely solo professionals to being members of larger organizations that are more intently focused on business and bottom-line concerns. This has caused enormous conflicts between their professional and economic motivations. Institutional providers, mainly hospitals, face similar pressures and conflicts. We believe that the training, professional ethic, and market behavior of these physicians mirrors in many significant ways the training, values, and behavior of faculty members, and that hospitals resemble institutions of higher education in many basic respects.

The Diversity and Needs of Consumers Are Changing

Consumers of health care services are the patients who demand and receive services from individual professionals and institutional providers. Their counterparts in higher education are the students. As we shall see, variety in the needs, capabilities, and motivations of patients is quite varied, as is their access to the health care services they need and want. We suspect the same can be said about the growing diversity of the population of student consumers of higher education services.

Government Is a Significant Presence in the Industry

Federal and state governments are a major source of health care funding. They establish tax and other policy incentives that shape and direct the market, they fund research that leads to new technologies and expectations of availability, and they establish the elements of a social contract in which the value of health and health care services is articulated. Increasingly, government at all levels has become a more active and influential factor in higher education as well. Although government action in the health care arena often lacks nimbleness, it rarely lacks influence. Could the same be true in higher education, as public policies direct more aspects of educational practice and federal student aid becomes an increasingly large share of institutional funding?

Technology Is a Major Driver of Change

Technology is the major driver of almost everything that happens in health care, from new drug therapies to microsurgery, diagnostic procedures that increase treatment success, and information technologies that may enable better management of disease, patients, and money. Combined with enhancements in telecommunications capacity, the increasing digitalization of health care procedures and information may offer significant opportunities to deliver quality health care services in new and dispersed settings. Technology is also a major factor in the evolution of delivery and management of higher education products—but, as with health care, not without the substantial restructuring of basic professional and institutional arrangements.

This initial picture highlighting the parallel characteristics of the health care and higher education industries strongly suggests that a better understanding of emergent trends in higher education can be gained by examination of the revolutionary changes that have rocked health care in the past 30 years.

3.3 HEALTH CARE: FROM COTTAGE INDUSTRY TO BIG BUSINESS

The watershed point that initiated the revolution in American health care was the enactment of Medicare in 1965. That legislation opened the doors of doctors' offices and hospitals to millions of elderly citizens who had previously been unable to pay for services; it inserted the government into the health care market and, in so doing, revealed in a new way the reality of cost-shifting. By politicizing health care, decisions that the government made about payments, services, and quality of care became, because of the sheer bulk of the Medicare (and later Medicaid) programs, major drivers for change in all aspects of the system. Medicare now accounts for over 20 percent of all U.S. health care expenditures and over 30 percent of hospital costs. In what follows, therefore, we will take the pre-Medicare era as the starting point for describing the changes that have shaped, and continue to reshape, health care delivery.

We believe that higher education may soon face a similar watershed point. Even a casual review of some of the major changes that have occurred in the health care delivery system, along with the possible implications of those changes for the future of higher education, suggests that profound change may be just around the corner. These parallels are summarized in Exhibit 3–4 and elaborated in the remainder of this section.

Health Care Providers: From Practitioners to Managers

Pre-Medicare physician practices in the United States were usually solo and small group practices that dealt with patients directly on a fee-for-service basis. Physicians, assisted by small office staffs or nurses, dealt as independent practitioners with patients, being reimbursed primarily in a fee-for-service way that encouraged overutilization of services. A referral system in which patients self-selected (often rationed by income and insurance) care from a variety of primary care and specialist providers led to uncoordinated care, especially for the elderly and chronically ill. There was little or no coordinated medical management of the patient's total case or professional review of the appropriateness of services provided, short of the occasional malpractice suit for egregious error, whether real or perceived.

In the current system, medical practice is quickly moving away from an era of solo and even small group practices. The financial pressures of maintaining the overhead structure now required to satisfy multiple payers and managers of care simply have made small practices economically unattractive. The growth of managed care coverage has forced physicians to contract with multiple plans to maintain patient volumes, and these multiple arrangements overwhelm small practices. As a result, solo practitioners are now affiliating with larger,

Exhibit 3–4
DEFINING CHARACTERISTICS OF HEALTH CARE CHANGE

Providers: From Practitioners to Managers

Health Care Before	Health Care Now	Higher Education Implications
• Independent "professionals" on fee-for-service reimbursement controlled utilization and costs • Specialists dominant force in decision making • Little professional review of services appropriateness • Few outcome measures collected and applied	• Moving to end of solo and even small group practices; more physicians are salaried employees • Primary care gate keeper role under direction of managed care organizations • Increased use of non-physicians to deliver services • Pressures to reduce specialists' utilization and costs • Fees now either heavily discounted, capitated or contracted • Increasing use of protocols or practice guidelines to prescribe care patterns • Restrictions on ownership of auxiliary services	• Faculty independence and control of academic standards and content may be challenged • New balance between specialized and generalists or between research versus teaching? • More critical review of outputs and outcomes • Tenured faculty positions replaced with adjuncts • Increased faculty organization and unionization

(continued)

often multiple-specialty groups, or becoming salaried employees of health maintenance organizations (HMOs) or physician or hospital-owned group practice organizations.

This move to managed care has also required primary care providers to take a more active gatekeeper role in the management of patients under their care. In some cases this role is incentivized through the use of capitation contracts that put the physician group at risk for all the care their patients require. In other instances, managed care contracts may require primary care physician referrals for all or most specialist care.

Along with these changes, the use of clinical protocols or disease management programs that provide specific guidelines and standards for

Exhibit 3–4
(Continued)

Institutions: From Passive to Active . . . and Tense		
Health Care Before	**Health Care Now**	**Higher Education Implications**
• Many hospitals, medical schools were local and non-profit • Payments mostly based on costs and charges • Relationships were not complex • Significant over-capacity	• Reduction of hospitals and beds • Increase of national chains and regional alliances • Fewer non-profit hospitals • Hospitals trying to be anchors of integrated systems • Declining use as care shifts to outpatient and ambulatory • Declining reimbursement—little fee-for-service left, no one pays charges	• Growth of non-traditional forms of ownership and governance • Pressure on less successful or poorer institutions to close or merge • New entrants —businesses establish and run internal education programs — i.e., Motorola University, or provide targeted endowments • More scrutiny of academic operation • Reengineering and streamlining to control costs and ensure quality • No truly integrated delivery system yet

physicians to follow when treating patients is spreading rapidly. Starting as proscribed drug formularies, these programs have now expanded to include a wide variety of cases and diagnoses. Some are imposed by managed care and other payers and enforced through judgment of what is "medically necessary" and therefore eligible for reimbursement. Other protocols are developed and adopted by physicians themselves (especially when they are at risk for the financial implications of treatment decisions). Though initially denounced as "cookbook medicine," many physicians have begun to recognize both economic and clinical value in these protocols and guidelines, and their development and application is now a major thrust in all aspects of medical practice.

These trends have culminated in a dramatic change in the role of the physician, from a detached professional who paid relatively little attention to the business aspects of the practice of medicine to a business owner and manager paying more active and aggressive attention to the economics of

Exhibit 3–4
(Continued)

Consumers: From Trusting Patients to Educated Consumers

Health Care Before	Health Care Now	Higher Education Implications
• Most workers covered by large employer-paid indemnity plans • Many elderly had poor coverage and access to health care insurance and services • System wide, high expenditures with relatively low average health status outcomes compared to other industrial countries	• Employer provided coverage move to managed care • Medicare and Medicaid have substantially increased access and buying power • Working uninsured are a major concern • Compared to other countries, less "official" rationing of care as an access control measure—although some occurring in the marketplace	• More diversity of students — older , mid-career • Students less willing and likely to attend full time and continuously • Improved access through distributed methodology and new technologies • Greater access to student loans and guaranteed tuition funds

(continued)

health care.[4] The impact of all these changes is reflected in reduced levels of physician satisfaction with their careers. A 1995 study found that 55 percent of physicians believed that the health care system had gotten worse, not better, in the past year. Physicians practicing in states with high managed-care penetration were more likely to be unhappy than their brethren in low-penetration states. Almost a quarter of surveyed physicians were dissatisfied with their current practice.[5]

This growing dissatisfaction with moving from a professional to a business orientation in the practice of medicine may well foreshadow a similar impact on faculty members, as the prevailing professional paradigm that centers responsibility for defining teaching, research, and certification criteria on individual professional judgment shifts to ac-

---

[4]For a good example of how these changes have been happening in one community, see Monica Langley, "Hospitals and Doctors Fight for Same Dollars in a Louisiana Town," *Wall Street Journal*, November 25, 1997, at 1.

[5]Karen Donelan et. al., "The New Medical Marketplace: Physicians Views," *Health Affairs*, September-October 1997, 139–48.

Exhibit 3–4
(Continued)

Payers: Market Clout Forces Improvements in Cost and Quality		
Health Care Before	**Health Care Now**	**Higher Education Implications**
• Many small payers with little leverage • Government not a significant factor except to encourage these trends through tax policy and funds for hospital beds • Most consumers had employer-supplied Indemnity coverage, provided no efficiency incentive to providers or consumers	• Government accounts for large share of the health care dollar, sets rates and patterns in Federal and state programs • Large employers and government are exercising more leverage on providers and insurers • Small employers become more active participants in the health care market through marketing alliances • Managed care has inserted a new agent between payers and providers and consumers • Politicization of health care—"disease of the month"	• Federal government an increasing factor — bringing new regulatory and political overhead • Competition and group purchasing through new financing arrangements leads to discounting • Risk and selection effects as institutions seek to identify and recruit full payers • Employers pay a larger share as more mid-career students are enrolled

commodate more business and market-sensitive concerns. The tenure system that underlies and reflects this professional ethic is under serious challenge in many institutions, and is being sidestepped in others as adjunct and part-time faculty spots replace tenure-track positions.

Institutions: From Passive to Active . . . and Tense

The past 30 years have been marked by revolutionary changes in the hospital segment of the health care system. The changes have significantly affected the complexity, ownership, economics, and community role of contemporary hospitals. With the introduction of new technologies and increasing service delivery in ambulatory settings, the number of available hospital beds in the United States has declined by

Exhibit 3–4
(Continued)

Technology: Facilitating Change and the "End Run"

Health Care Before	Health Care Now	Higher Education Implications
• Low technology business • More reliance on "Marcus Welby" as medical ideal • No information technology • Health care a set of discrete events, not coordinated patient information of care management understanding	• Very high tech and expensive new interventions • Many developments in information technology, but still lots to do to bring the information needs under control— failure of CHIN initiatives • Major privacy and usage issues hamper incorporation of state-of-the-art information systems • Relatively low return on technology in terms of average health status measures so far	• Pressure to incorporate new information technologies will make major change in the nature of instruction and learning • New information technologies will change emphasis from teaching to learning— more student empowerment • Possibilities of distance learning create more national market, will change internal governance arrangements

(continued)

almost 15 percent in the last decade. Average daily census is about half what it was in 1960. This decline has occurred despite the fact that the older population, which uses more intensive hospital services, has been growing substantially. Average length of stay for hospital admissions is down from 7.3 days in 1985 to 5.8 in 1995, although the future average may well begin to increase as most nonintensive treatments move to outpatient settings. Hospitals increasingly diversify the products they offer in order to remain financially viable, adding outpatient services and nonacute beds to the traditional mix of inpatient services. These medical changes make the hospital a more complex institution, with new strategies for capturing patients and new alliances with and ownership of physician groups to ensure a steady flow of revenue-generating patients. Hospitals now engage in active marketing, product development, and advertising to attract doctors and patients.

Along with these dramatic changes in hospital use have come changes in hospital ownership and governance. Today, 12 percent of

Exhibit 3–4
(Continued)

Systems: Making Market Rationalization Possible

Health Care Before	Health Care Now	Higher Education Implications
• Little integration of service delivery • Substantial overlap of service—not viewed as a market for the most part	• Various attempts to develop integrated delivery systems—the markets are still developing as participants try new arrangements • Very local based depending on penetration of managed care • Growth of large, vertically integrated systems generates requirements for investor money—increases sensitivity to non-health system incentives	• Buyers and payers and consumers will demand better coordination and less competition to save money • Reduce duplication and overlap • Higher education becomes a commodity • Innovative delivery systems could emerge to deal with multiple and changing demands

hospital beds are managed by for-profit entities, compared to 8 percent in 1975,[6] and conversions from nonprofits increase annually. In addition, for-profit hospitals were among the first to pursue Integrated Delivery Systems (IDSs) and Physician Hospital Organizations (PHOs), viewed by many as the forerunners of the Provider Sponsored Organizations (PSOs) enfranchised to accept risk for Medicare patients by the 1997 Balanced Budget Act.

A major consequence of the emergence of integrated hospital chains is that these large national companies require significant capital to fund their expansion and acquisitions. The source of that capital is Wall Street—and with that capital infusion comes control and a set of demands on management that often is at odds with the traditional concerns of hospital boards and administrators. Rather than focusing on community health needs and quality of care delivered, the pressures of the capital markets can cause these companies to concentrate more on

[6]*American Hospital Association Hospital Statistics*, 1996-97 ed.

return on investments, short-term bottom-line results, and the opinions of market and industry analysts.

Changes in the method of reimbursement for hospital services have reduced the amount of revenue hospitals are able to generate and have also changed the incentive systems. Thirty years ago, most hospital stays were reimbursed based on "customary and reasonable" charges (albeit with discounts for high-volume third-party payers such as Blue Shield). In 1983, Medicare—which alone is responsible for 30 percent of all hospital charges—changed its reimbursement methodology to a diagnosis-based flat rate. Other payers have also moved away from paying based on charges, preferring to negotiate capitation or per-diem rates. These reimbursement changes were incentives for hospitals to change from providing an increasing number of separately billed services to finding ways to economize and streamline the costs of care.[7] The excess of bed capacity in most markets, which forced hospitals to compete aggressively to cover the variable costs of hospital stays, has facilitated this movement. Excess bed capacity, which contributes to high fixed costs, has been reduced by closing units and converting these facilities to other uses (outpatient and ambulatory surgery centers, long term care, etc.), and has been a staple of the acquisition strategies of large national chains.

The much-publicized missteps of one of these large health care conglomerates are unlikely to portend the end of the consolidation era. National providers with national access and standards, marketed with national brands, are only a short distance away.

The hospital, once a neutral setting in which independent physicians provided services to patients with little overall control or direction, has become an aggressive and competing business with objectives and interests in tension with those of the physicians who deliver services. Traditionally, the university provided a similar neutral setting in which individual faculty and departments could pursue their own teaching and research. Now the same economic and other forces that have transformed the hospital area are also knocking at the gates of the American university.

Consumers: From Trusting Patients to Educated Consumers

The introduction of employer-paid health insurance (which grew substantially during World War II in large part as a means of reducing increases in cash wages) is the primary distinguishing and driving characteristic of consumer behavior in the health care market. The avail-

---

[7]This change in cost-saving incentives has in turn contributed to the growth in use of information technology as a means of tracking and controlling the cost of providing care for which the price is essentially fixed. See § 3.6.

ability of insurance to most working families meant that few people actually paid for their health services at the point of care. Thus, most consumers still have little incentive to apply their usual economic rationale to health care purchases. The special nature of health care services, especially the very real life-or-death nature of many choices, has meant that consumer behavior has been difficult to predict or affect. When the costs of care are not directly visible, consumers have a tendency to overuse health care services. In a fee-for-service environment, in which providers have incentives to provide additional services, the economic effects are substantial. The results were that the United States had the highest per-capita health care costs of any industrial nation, and those costs have been rising much faster than inflation for most of the last three decades.

Exacerbating the problem was the fact that before Medicare and Medicaid, many elderly, poor, and disabled Americans excluded from the employment-based insurance system had little or no insurance coverage and limited access to health care services. The Health Care Financing Administration (HCFA) estimates that over half of the elderly had no health insurance coverage before Medicare. Those without any coverage, as well as those with only limited coverage and financial means, relied on family or charity for the cost of their care. The real cost of charity care was then shifted to the paying population in the form of higher charges.

With the introduction of Medicare and Medicaid, the number of uncovered elderly, poor, and disabled fell dramatically. However, because Medicare and Medicaid have limited benefits and often substantial cost-sharing requirements, complete access to health care services still is a problem for many Americans. In addition, almost 20 percent of all workers do not have employer-provided insurance, and that number is growing as many employers (especially small ones) opt not to provide or pay for coverage.

The changes in health care financing led to rapid increases in health care costs and increasing pressure from government and employers to keep cost growth under control. Movement to managed care has restrained cost growth for the years 1995 to 1998, but has resulted in increased frustration among consumers who are now faced with a bewildering array of choices of plans, organizations, benefits, and cost-sharing options from which to choose. Traditional relationships between patients and providers have been disrupted. Consumer reaction to these changes has become dramatic and often takes the form of political activity, such as the reaction to the famous Harry and Louise advertisements that played a major role in undermining public support for the Clinton health reform initiatives. More recently, consumers have pressed for legislative reactions to media reports of outpatient mastectomies and inappropriately quick discharges after childbirth. Finding the developing managed care system to be nonresponsive to their needs, many consumers are demanding changes in the way the system operates, to improve access, choice, and quality. Managed care companies, physicians, hospitals, public officials, and employers are responding to these consumer demands by offering new products, increased availability of information, and attention to patient service.

Payers: Market Clout Forces Improvements in Cost and Quality

The concept of insurance is based on spreading the risk of high costs across a large population. However, consumers' expectations for health insurance have evolved over time from protection against catastrophic costs to coverage of all routine health care services. This change has also contributed to the rapid growth in health care costs. The magnitude of the separation of consumers from the cost of health care is illustrated by the fact that in 1960, 55 percent of all personal health care expenditures were made out-of-pocket by consumers. By 1995, that figure had declined to 20.8 percent, with the increase in private health insurance and government accounting for most of the difference (see Exhibit 3–5).

But if consumers do not have any direct contact with the costs of the services they receive, those paying the bill—employers and government—have felt the pressure of rapidly rising health care costs and have reacted by trying to control utilization and costs. These efforts have taken many forms, from raising the share of health care premiums paid by employees, to instituting various forms of cost-sharing (copayments and deductibles), to using managed care approaches to control utilization and restrain costs. Moreover, payers are beginning to exer-

Exhibit 3–5
PERCENTAGE CHANGES IN SOURCES OF HEALTH CARE PAYMENTS

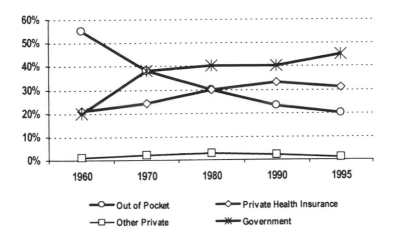

cise discipline over providers and insist that performance and quality be valued as much as cost reductions.

There have been similar significant shifts in the revenue sources of higher education (see Exhibit 3–6). Over the past two decades, the percentage of total costs covered by tuition and fees has increased for all categories of institutions. At the same time, the contributions of governments have decreased—substantially for state governments. In part, the reduction of government funding for higher education represents transfers of those funds to pay for the large increases in government health care costs noted earlier. The increased burden being shifted to tuition has already begun to have an impact on consumers similar to the cost increases in health care. Parents and students are beginning to question the value of the added costs; universities and colleges have been forced to adopt pricing strategies that include significant discounting (principally through financial aid) in order to compete, and have been forced to begin administrative reform and reengineering to reduce cost growth.

Technology: Facilitating Change and the "End-Run"

Perhaps the most vivid way to characterize the dramatic effect that improved medical technology has had on health care is to compare media representations then and now: *Marcus Welby, M.D.* versus *E.R.* What had been a relatively low-tech endeavor only a generation ago has now become dominated by all the wonders of modern medicine we take for granted. The effects have been to extend life for the millions of patients who have received transplants, open-heart surgery, or

Exhibit 3–6
SOURCES OF HIGHER EDUCATION FUNDING—
PERCENTAGE DISTRIBUTIONS

	Universities				Colleges			
	Private		Public		Private		Public	
	1977	1994	1977	1994	1977	1994	1977	1994
Tuition/Fees	40%	45%	16%	24%	62%	70%	16%	24%
Federal	30%	22%	20%	19%	12%	7%	17%	14%
State and Local	4%	3%	54%	43%	3%	4%	63%	51%
Private Gifts	13%	14%	5%	8%	16%	11%	2%	5%
Endowment	8%	8%	1%	1%	6%	6%	0%	1%
Sales/Services	5%	8%	4%	5%	1%	2%	2%	5%
	100%	100%	100%	100%	100%	100%	100%	100%

Source: National Center for Education Statistics

the latest chemotherapy. Millions more have been spared painful and invasive procedures through the use of new drug therapies, space-age diagnostic methods, and refined surgical techniques. Costs have increased accordingly to pay for these breakthroughs—sometimes from overuse, certainly from extending the lives of patients who otherwise would not have survived, and proportionally to spread development costs over all services and products.

Information technology in many ways has and will continue to have the most profound effect on health care delivery. At one end of the information spectrum, new computer-driven imaging technologies and available bandwidth are making medical interventions much more precise and efficient, even at great distances. Improvements in computer processing underlie the unfolding fields of genetic and molecular biology that will revolutionize treatment in the future. For our present purposes, though, the most important aspect of the information age in health care is the ability to better organize and manage the vast health care enterprise. The promise of computerized patient records, shared among all providers treating a patient, will allow medicine to move from being a set of discrete events to being coordinated patient care and management.

As with all new technologies, information sciences are expensive and difficult to integrate into an increasingly cost-sensitive existing practice. Despite billions of dollars invested in health care information systems, we are still far from achieving the expected outcomes in either patient care or system management. Issues of privacy, system compatibility, institution and provider resistance, and oversold technology have made success much more difficult than expected.

The lesson for higher education is clear. Technology holds great promise to improve the efficiency of higher education management, teaching, and learning, but change will come only slowly and at a higher price than expected. That cost will not be measured only in dollars, but also in profound changes in prevailing values and the sacrifice of some sacred cows of the academic environment. At the same time, some "end-runs" are likely, in which new providers of direct training and then education (along the lines of Microsoft, IBM, Sylvan Learning, or a cable mega-company) will capture a measurable share of the current college and university market, by exploiting the power and cost-effectiveness of new information and communication technologies without the transition costs and dislocations that existing traditional institutions face.

Systems: Making Market Rationalization Possible

As we have said, health care 30 years ago can be fairly described as a collection of local cottage industries. There was little integration of services or providers. Often patients were forced to navigate themselves through the various sources of care. Physicians operated as low-capitalized independent practitioners. Hospitals were mostly loosely managed, community-based institutions in which administration played second fiddle to the medical staff.

As managed care systems, for-profit hospital chains, and pressures to control costs have increased, the health care industry has developed a much more complex set of relationships and systems. New forms of ownership and governance have emerged, bringing with them new motivations (especially from investors) for the calculations and considerations of health care managers. The market now contains various attempts to develop integrated delivery systems, from those locally based to national corporations that own hundreds of hospitals or manage care for millions of consumers. With the pressure to bring managed care aggressively into Medicare, even more system mergers and new alliances will evolve.

The initial movement to managed care by new entities was to "managed funding." As the systems have grown and evolved, a real trend to manage care as the way to manage dollars is occurring. This change has come slowly, through new technologies, new measurement opportunities, and new accountability—the acceptance of quality standards and financial risk for the care provided.

Higher education systems mirror in many ways the early development of integrated networks and arrangements in health care. As with health care, education reflects enormous duplication of effort, isolation, and failure to address broad issues of resource allocation. The lesson from health care is that the changes that move service delivery to more integrated systems are inevitable; they result from the continuing pressures of consumers and payers, and eventually from the cutting-edge institutions of the education establishment itself.

3.4 DRIVERS OF CHANGE

Change in a market and for a product as complex as health care is always multidimensional. These complexities were described earlier. There is no single factor that explains how and why health care arrangements and systems evolve. We will attempt, in this section, to briefly isolate and highlight some of the major underlying factors that have driven and continue to drive the health care system changes described previously. In many instances we believe that these same forces will change how higher education is financed and operated.

The first major factor is that cost growth forced payers to seek savings and get organized to shape the system. As the costs of health care continued to escalate in the 1970s and 1980s, the two major sources of those payments—government and employers—began to take action. Climbing Medicare expenditures, reflecting delivery of more and more intensive services to a growing aging population that was living longer, generated political concerns as to how to control the costs of those programs. Attempts to solve the problem by raising patient costs and controlling access met with fierce political opposition from well-organized coalitions. Medicare was able to institute some savings, and generate major changes in provider incentives, by moving from reimbursement of hospitals by charges and costs to Diagnosis Related Groups (DRGs) that provide flat payments (based on average costs and lengths of stay) depending on the cause of hospitalization. This change removed the incentive to keep patients in the hospital longer than needed and shifted the attention of hospital staffs to improving efficiency and cost savings by reducing lengths of stay and resources used. This in turn (along with rapid changes in technology) led to development of a wide range of ambulatory centers and clinics, both hospital-based and freestanding. Changing funding methodologies can have profound impacts on institutions and service delivery, and this lesson should not be lost on higher education, where new payment mechanisms and funding sources will undoubtedly have major ripple effects across the university system.

Another government response in the 1970s was activity to encourage the development of new forms of health care delivery and payment. Although the HMO Act of 1972 was not immediately successful in spawning a multitude of new forms of organizations to have a systemic impact on health care delivery and costs, the incentives and lessons of that early period were very influential 10 years later as the health care market began to shift in very basic ways.

Employers, the second major source of health care funding, were less constrained by politics in their responses to the growing burden of health care costs. American businesses spent almost $250 billion on health care in 1995. Some (particularly smaller firms) began cutting those costs by reducing or dropping coverage, or by raising employees' share of the costs. Others looked to new methods of providing some discipline in employee use of health care services—the beginning of the growth of managed care insurance products. These new financial arrangements typically put more responsibility on the insurance provider to control costs by instituting systems of review and approval before employees could receive some care. In the period from 1988 to 1997, the percentage of employees covered by some form of managed care increased from 29 percent to 81 percent. Employers have truly moved the health care market in major ways in a very short time. They (and other payers and consumers) could reshape the finances and management of education just as quickly.

The movement to managed care has had notable consequences. Consumers used to relative freedom of choice as to their providers and treatments have responded with anger at some of the tactics and operations of the new care managers. Some of this anger has been aimed (and orchestrated) at specific managed care policies, such as limited hospital stays for maternity cases (so-called *drive-thru deliveries*), and has led to a number of legislative proposals and legislation in both federal and state legislatures directed at establishing specific standards for managed care plans. The controversies generated by managed care plans also led to the establishment of a Presidential Advisory Commission that has now recommended a Health Care Consumer Bill of Rights.[8]

The growth of managed care also led to an increase in concern about establishing and measuring standards for the outcomes of health care. This movement has taken two forms. Increasing attention is being paid to development of clinical standards and protocols to define appropriate medical practice. In response to the wide variation in treatment and outcomes, medical care practices and plans, government agencies, and professional associations have begun to develop, publish, and implement detailed clinical guidelines that are evidence-based practices in diagnosis and treatment. Secondly, payers (and to a lesser extent consumers) have begun to collect and publish detailed data on health care system performance. These report cards, especially the Health Plan Employer Data and Information Set (HEDIS), are enabling buyers to compare and evaluate the performance of plans as they make purchase and enrollment decisions.

Demands for greater accountability from higher education, and demands to measure the outputs and return on educational investment, are already starting to increase. As with health care, it may be inevitable that one result of these demands will be to separate the measurement of outcomes and quality from the provision of these services. New independent (and often employer-focused) organizations are taking the control of these measures away from the doctors and hospitals. The period in which faculty and administration will be able to both deliver services and be the sole evaluator of the quality of those services may be limited.

As costs grew, buyer concern generated new payment mechanisms, control structures, and organizational entities. The consolidation and privatization of the hospital system described earlier forced these entities to compete for a shrinking number of inpatient days, and to strengthen their source of admissions by developing alliances with the physician providers who more directly controlled admissions. In some cases these alliances were partnerships between the institutions and independent physicians and groups. In some markets, hospitals began buying up physician practices in an effort to build the vertical integration that would ensure patient flow. In others, vertical integration failed and is being replaced by virtual

[8]Advisory Commission on Consumer Protection and Quality in the Health Care Industry, "Consumer Bill of Rights and Responsibilities: Report to the President of the United States," November 1997.

integration—organizations of hospitals, providers, and insurers that remain independent but enter into a series of contractual arrangements designed to achieve better coordination and effectiveness.

The marketplace of health plans and provider organizations has also been stimulated by the other changes in the financing and institutional arenas. Partly in response to the growing role of hospitals in the ownership and direction of physician practices, and partly in reaction to the growing involvement of traditional insurance payers in utilization management (the practice of grading what is and is not reimbursable), new varieties of physician organizations began to emerge. Some were simply consolidations of previously independent practices that merged to achieve better market penetration, economies of scale, and negotiating position with payers and hospitals. Organizations such as the Voluntary Hospital Association (VHA) and Premiere Inc., each owned by a small group of hospitals but serving a broad array of the not-for-profit hospital market, have pioneered savings in purchases and technologies for their member systems.

Others began accepting some risk for the health care costs and services provided to enrolled patients; these took a variety of forms and have had a mixed record of success. What had been a simple marketplace became crowded and confusing, with insurance companies, managed care companies, hospital-based integrated systems, HMOs, IPAs, PPOs, PHOs, and other new forms blurring the traditional lines between payers and providers. Recently, large regional and national HMOs have begun to merge and combine to form mega-companies. As the shakeout continues, fewer and fewer locally based delivery systems remain, but the development of new variations and modifications continues unabated.

This growing consolidation and organizational transformation generates the need for capital: to buy individual practices, to develop and execute marketing plans, to purchase the powerful information systems required to meet the efficiency needs of these new forms of health care delivery, and in some cases to fund reserves to meet state insurance requirements. The active participants themselves are not often able to meet the enormous capital requirements and thus are forced to turn to outside investors and stockholders to finance the new ventures.[9]

---

[9]The capital needs have been exacerbated as formerly nonprofit institutions and insurers (Blue Cross plans) convert to for-profit status, transferring huge amounts of capital that might have been used to finance this growth to new nonprofit community foundations. More than $9 billion has been transferred to these new foundations in the last few years. Untold more dollars have gone to executives of those companies who were able to assume ownership at (often) fire-sale prices. See S. Issacs, D. Beatrice, and W. Carr, "Health Care Conversion Foundations: A Status Report," *Health Affairs* 16, no. 6 (November-December 1997): 228–36.

With this influx of investor capital comes new controls and demands on the managers and staff of these firms. Rather than being accountable to a community board of directors or to individual patients, these new health care corporations are more attuned to the needs and demands of Wall Street analysts and traders, whose concerns are mostly for their own bottom lines. This has forced these companies to focus more on bottom-line, short-term results, potentially undermining the level of commitment to quality health care services.

3.5 PARALLELS TO HIGHER EDUCATION: THE MARKET ASSAULTS THE IVORY TOWER

The Providers: Faculty and Institutions

The primary providers of higher education services are the faculty members who have direct contact with students, develop the individual courses and the overall curriculum, establish and administer requirements for certification, and produce the knowledge base that is then transmitted to students. Most faculty hold or aspire to Ph.D. degrees. Few faculty have any formal training in education or learning theory; instead, their pedagogical practices are largely based on replaying what they experienced as students. For many faculty, teaching is the price they must pay to enjoy the life of research and writing they really prize.

It is not surprising, given this context, that higher education has evolved as teacher-centered rather than learner-centered. Students have been expected to conform to faculty schedules and priorities. For instance, they can take courses (i.e., learn) only when the faculty are free to offer the courses that the faculty have determined to be required. This of course parallels health care, which is doctor-centered rather than patient-centered. Physicians are trained to deal with disease, not patients. It has only been in the past few years that the increasingly competitive markets for health care services have forced providers to begin being more customer-conscious and to focus on preventive services as well as treatments.

While faculty delivery of the educational product has been resistant to change (particularly to new learning technologies, as we will discuss later), the institutions of higher education have been resistant to the management revolution. Over the past two or more decades, businesses (including health care) have been concerned with improving the quality, timeliness, and cost-effectiveness of their products and processes. Pushed by competitive markets, companies have exploited new technologies and methods to produce products and services better, faster, and cheaper. Whole industries have sprung up emphasizing customer service as the key, from mail order sales and electronic commerce, to "just in time" delivery schedules, to information services. Until recently, however, universities have been immune to these trends.

Now the buyers and payers for higher education are beginning to demand more. At least 27 state legislatures have established commissions or study groups to review the performance of public higher education systems. Largely in response to costs that are growing much faster than inflation, and an inability on the part of the universities to quantify the value they add for the funds they receive, both public and private institutions are starting to incorporate the management tools now common in the commercial world to evaluate their own operations.

As some writers (notably William Massey, Michael Hooker, and Molly Brand in this volume) have noted, what may be occurring is a more profound paradigm shift, similar to what has occurred in health care. That shift will require that faculties and institutions reexamine very basic principles that govern how they operate and respond to their various stakeholders.

- Will employers demand certification of competency rather than credit hours?

- Will boards of directors insist that classroom seats be allocated based on net revenues?

- Will students seek out a university that allows them to design a virtual curriculum in which they take the best courses from any university or college around the nation or the world?

- Will Microsoft or the Library of Congress build a virtual library that eliminates the repository library funded by most universities and colleges today?

- Will an educational magnate buy the contracts of the 400 best professors in America and offer a world-class degree for one-half the price of a Harvard or Yale education?

- Will guaranteed tuition pools bargain not only for discounted tuition rates, but also for performance warranties that guarantee graduates the ability to land a job at a reasonable salary level?

- Will the marketplace require quality processes and outcome measurement as core operating principles of higher education?[10]

[10]For a particularly cogent statement of these issues, see the Remarks to the National Commission on the Cost of Higher Education by William F. Massey at the September 7–8, 1997 meeting of the Commission. Also see Michael Hooker, "The Transformation of Higher Education," in *The Learning Revolution* edited by Diane C. Oblinger and Sean C. Rush (Bolton, Mass.: Anker Publishing, 1997).

Market forces very similar to these have caused huge upheavals in the health care system in recent years, with significant turmoil and pain both for those who resisted and those who embraced change.

The Buyers: "Just-in-Time" Education

In addition to the cost and productivity factors that are now beginning to reshape higher education, substantial changes in the numbers, types, and needs of students are creating profound changes in the demand for education. No longer is the university catering mostly to 18- to 22-year-old students. Now the average age of students in all forms of higher education is over 25. Education is increasingly being understood as a lifelong activity, not one that ends at age 22 or 26. As the economy becomes even more knowledge-based, and as the content of that knowledge changes at even faster rates, ongoing education will be mandatory for economic and personal success. As institutions of higher education gain more part-time students, as more educational demands come from employers and adults for mid-career education and training, new forms of education delivery and content will be required. How must higher education change and adapt to meet those new needs?

The experience of the health care system suggests that institutional response will be driven by basic market and political forces, which will increasingly differentiate the institutional providers and will pressure them to change or lose their market share and identities through closing or merging. Pressures to focus on quality and customer needs will draw new players into the market, and these new entrants (not unlike the much-touted University of Phoenix, as well as company-operated institutions such as Motorola University) will magnify the pressures on existing institutions to change. As universities become more sensitive to customer (tuition-payer) needs, they will respond by differentiating their products, seeking economies and more quality-based processes, and incorporating technologies that allow them to be more student- and learning-focused. New partnerships will develop as the business community and government make their needs felt in the choices of how they recruit and train new generations of knowledge workers.

Responding to the Market: Platinum Cards, "Wannabes," and Entrepreneurs

William Massey of the National Center for Postsecondary Improvement has characterized institutions of higher education as belonging to one of three categories:

- The small number of prestige institutions that compete on the basis of visibility and image, usually based on faculty research, with durability in the market based on traditional educational values

- Prestige-seeking institutions that aspire to the elite category but lack the market power to achieve that status

- Educational reputation institutions that are attempting to build a market niche by catering to student needs, and whose market potential depends on delivering quality as defined by the customers, as opposed to more traditional academic values[11]

The parallels to hierarchies of medical institutions are striking. Top-tier academic medical centers represent the cutting edge in research, treatment, and training, and are relatively immune to some aspects of market competition—but they are a poor model for other hospitals and delivery systems that have had to become much more market-sensitive. A major issue for national and local health care policy makers is just how many very specialized (and high-cost) hospitals we really need. Should every community hospital be equipped and funded to perform open-heart surgery? How many expensive MRIs are needed? In the same vein, how many top-level research universities are needed? Should every institution seek the same mix of teaching and research, or produce Ph.D. graduates (many of whom will not find jobs that use their specific skills)?

In the growing differentiated market for higher education, pricing strategies will be a central factor. In examining health care we discussed the evolution of new forms of payment as the market grew more complex, and as the market increasingly used price strategies to affect the mode and organization of service delivery. The same phenomenon seems to be happening in higher education. Despite high tuition bills (and even higher rates of growth), elite institutions have engaged in a form of price discounting through their financial aid programs. As corporations and governments increase their purchases of education services, they will undoubtedly demand different price (as well as substantive and delivery) processes. The growing use of prepaid tuition plans by state governments is another indication of the same trend.

[11]Massey, *supra* n. 10.

Technology: The Cost of "Zero Cost"

There is no doubt that the growing power and availability of information technologies will be a tremendous force in moving higher education to new modes of delivery and organization. Attracted by the technological promise, as well as the apparently low marginal costs, of these new technologies, major programs in computerized learning systems, distance learning, and use of telecommunications are creating new opportunities for improving the performance of higher education in an era when its effectiveness is under such broad challenge.

As the revolutionary adoption of technology in higher education continues, it is possible to imagine interactive distance learning replacing physical plants. National educational institutions become feasible. More control of educational content and delivery will pass from faculty to students, who will have greater ability to judge the utility and efficiency of different kinds of education and training. A few professors could teach all of America under high-paying contracts, replacing professors at local institutions who will assume more mentoring roles and work from a standardized and nationally delivered curriculum.

Massey and Zemsky have identified two major areas in which the introduction of more powerful information technologies can increase learning productivity: first, by enabling economies of scale (reduced cost per incremental student and reduced costs of incremental knowledge); and second, by allowing customization of delivery to better meet the individual needs of a wide variety of students.[12] As they acknowledge, though, introducing these new technologies will require revolutionary changes in the roles, values, and skills of faculty and administration. There will be substantial resistance, especially from faculty and academic departments who will face reductions in their numbers and changes in their roles and responsibilities. The costs of this new technology will be much greater than anyone estimates at the start, and the results, because they depend so much on changing attitudes and deeply held values, will be slower to mature than desired.

That resistance to expense and pace of change is remarkably similar to the experience in health care. Doctors and others have been slow to adapt their traditional roles to the new information age, especially in embracing the more coordinated practice of medicine and patient care that technology facilitates. But the change was inexorable—as it is in education—and is now under way, however costly. New data systems have proven very expensive and time-consuming to develop and install. A whole new industry of medical informatics has developed and

[12]William F. Massey and Robert Zemsky, *Using Information Technology to Enhance Academic Productivity* (Washington, D.C.: EDUCOM, 1995).

prospered, but so far it has failed to achieve the standardization and penetration to complete the transformation of health care to a truly information-driven industry. In the meantime, tricky issues such as the privacy of patient records, competing technologies, and incorporation of legacy data and systems all combine with the expected physician and institutional resistance to further delay what most see as an inevitable march.

3.6   THE PROGNOSIS: AS WITH HEALTH CARE, HIGHER EDUCATION HAS BECOME TOO IMPORTANT TO AVOID MARKET FORCES

Market forces based on technological change have had a dramatic impact well beyond health care and higher education. The demise of the Soviet Union, where there were no legitimized markets, is perhaps the most extreme example of this phenomenon. No matter how much the leaders of the Soviet Union wanted to compete in the world economy, they could not match the ability of market-based economies to produce goods, create capital, spur innovation, and allocate resources. Moreover, the power of virtually free and instantaneous information greatly reduced the ability of Soviet leaders to keep their citizens from knowing the better world that existed outside their walls.

Similarly, the power of technology and global capital has empowered the marketplace's assault on almost all aspects of American society. To name only a few, we are already witnessing immense changes in banking and finance, automobile manufacturing, real estate, postal and delivery systems, government operations, and the ways in which we spend our leisure time, in addition to health care.[13] There is every reason to believe that these market forces, while only lapping at the door of higher education now, will become forces of tidal dimension.

Indeed, just as health care is fundamental to survival and the quality of life, so education and training are becoming the key differentiators between those who live in relative wealth and those who live in poverty. Realizing this, students will continue to pay more and more attention to the cost/benefit equation in purchasing higher education, and will increasingly demand that higher education's claim of high

[13]This is not to say that these changes are without costs—many of them involving serious social and personal disruption—that must be addressed. The preceding discussions have noted many of the dislocations that have been evidenced in health care and are likely to be present as higher education becomes more subject to these same market and technology pressures.

quality be demonstrated by tangible evidence in the form of increased earning power and quality of life.

Although the transformation of health care is still a work in progress, we believe that the changes wrought by market forces embodied in technology, massive capital, and heightened consumer demand are illustrative and helpful in thinking about the future of higher education. The need to understand market forces, to creatively use technology, to deal with large capital pools, and to negotiate with demanding consumers will test the responsiveness and inventiveness of higher education. We have little doubt that higher education will be able to meet this challenge. Higher education has adapted in the past, and it is now so fundamental to the competitive advantage and wealth of our nation that consumers will demand change, and leaders within and without higher education will invest significantly in meeting these challenges.

Just as the health care industry has wrestled with its new relationship to the marketplace and technology, so higher education will grapple with these forces. During this time of change, the leaders of higher education may find both solace and insight from the changes occurring in the health care industry today.

Strategic Partnerships: What Universities and Corporations Can Do Together

MOLLY CORBETT BROAD

**President, The University of North Carolina
Former Executive Vice Chancellor, The California State
University**

4.1   INTRODUCTION

It has become a cliché to say that higher education must change to meet the challenges of the information economy, but that's probably because the statement is so obviously true. An unprecedented convergence of trends—demographic, economic, and social—is occurring that will require institutions of higher education to change in ways that, to this point, were considered impossible. The formation of strategic partnerships is a key adaptive response to this emerging new environment in higher education. Faced with a tidal wave of projected new enrollments, declining levels of state support, and the dramatic demands of the ever-accelerating information economy, colleges and universities will need to explore strategic relationships with many types of organizations in order to generate the resources and acquire the expertise necessary for surviving and thriving in the years ahead.

Nowhere is this perspective more true than in California, which continues to serve as the national laboratory for economic, social, and demographic trends and their effects on higher education. California is rapidly becoming a "majority minority" state, with both increasing ethnic diversity and sustained population growth in what is already the nation's most populous state. Meanwhile, its state government and many localities are still struggling to recover from California's greatest economic crisis since the Great Depression and the impact it has had on tax revenues and pent-up demand for public services. In response to these challenges, and with an eye to the opportunities they might offer, California State University began in 1993 to lay the foundation for pursuing the strategic partnerships that would be necessary for maintaining the vitality of the university and enhancing the quality of teaching and learning within it. Along the way, the CSU recognized the need to engage in a planning process for updating and expanding its technological capacities, realizing that meeting its needs in this area would require it to use its size and resulting economic leverage to engage major technology firms in strategic partnerships. The CSU experience illustrates both the value and the growing importance of strategic partnerships in the higher education setting.

4.2   FORCES DRIVING CHANGE

By now we have all read of the dramatic growth in the retirement-age population that will occur as the "baby boomer" generation continues to mature. By the year 2005, the preretirement segment of the population, ages 45 to 64, is expected to be roughly 19 million persons larger than it is today. What may have gone unnoticed is the significant increase in the K–16 age group projected to occur over this same time period, as the children of the boomers pass through the nation's educational system. An estimated 7 million more children will swell the ranks of this population segment by 2005, straining the capacity of the nation's school districts as well as its colleges and universities

Exhibit 4–1
SURGE IN THE SCHOOLS

Public school enrollment will surge over the next 10 years, especially in California, which is expecting almost a million more students.
States with the largest projected enrollment increases in public schools, 1997 to 2007 (in thousands), include:

State	Students in 1997	Students in 2007	Number of Additional Students	% Change
California	5,860	6,780	920	15.7%
Texas	3,900	4,314	414	10.6%
Georgia	1,358	1,502	144	10.6%
North Carolina	1,240	1,332	92	7.4%
Arizona	832	922	90	10.8%
Virginia	1,115	1,198	83	7.4%
Florida	2,300	2,372	72	3.1%
New York	2,902	2,965	63	2.2%
Tennessee	923	984	61	6.6%
Utah	488	543	55	11.3%

Source: U.S. Department of Education, National Center for Education Statisitcs, *Projections of Education Statistics to 2007.*

(see Exhibit 4–1).[1] California's institutions of higher education alone must prepare themselves for the surge in enrollments that will result as a projected 1 million additional students pass through the state's schools over the next decade.[2] Clark Kerr and others have dubbed this projected growth in enrollments "Tidal Wave II." Higher education, both nationally and in California, has not seen potential enrollment growth of this magnitude since the days of the GI Bill, and even in times of solid fiscal support its challenges would be daunting.

[1]U.S. Bureau of the Census, *Population Projections for States by Age, Sex, Race, and Hispanic Origin: 1995 to 2025,* October 1996.
[2]U.S. Department of Education, National Center for Education Statistics, *Projections of Education Statistics to 2007,* June 1997.

Exhibit 4–2
STATE APPROPRIATIONS FOR HIGHER EDUCATION
PER $1,000 OF PERSONAL INCOME—FY 1997

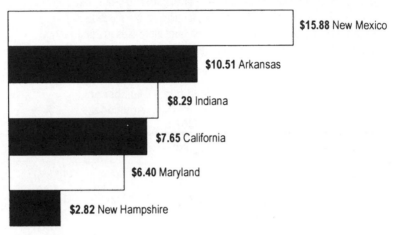

$15.88 New Mexico

$10.51 Arkansas

$8.29 Indiana

$7.65 California

$6.40 Maryland

$2.82 New Hampshire

U.S. Average = $7.65

Source: Mortenson Research Seminar, *Postsecondary Education Opportunity,* November 1996.

Unfortunately, if current trends continue, American higher education will have to confront this explosion in demand with declining state support. Nationally, state appropriations for higher education per $1,000 of personal income have declined from a peak of $11.22 in fiscal year (FY) 1979 to $7.65 in FY 1997, representing a loss of 31.8 percent over that time period. In California, the scene is even worse, with state appropriations per $1,000 of personal income plummeting from a high of $14.14 in FY 1980 to $7.65 in FY 1997, representing a decline of almost 46 percent. As a way of dramatically emphasizing this trend, a simple extrapolation of the recent pattern of experience would result in zero state appropriations for higher education in California as soon as 2015, with the rest of the nation crossing the "finish line" by 2035 (see Exhibit 4–2).[3] Although no one honestly believes that state support for higher education will totally disappear, these figures indicate the steepness of higher education's decline as a priority for state funding vis-à-vis corrections and health and welfare spending. Moreover, they illustrate the potentially traumatic implications of the continuing decline in state support for America's (and California's) colleges and universities.

[3]Mortenson Research Seminar, *Postsecondary Education Opportunity,* "State Tax Fund Appropriations for Higher Education for FY 1997 (and Beyond)," November 1996.

Even as state funding for higher education has declined, the importance of education to one's economic prospects has significantly increased. U.S. Department of Labor statistics indicate that an individual who has received a high school degree can expect to earn 33 percent more over her or his lifetime than someone who does not complete high school, and the value of postsecondary education is dramatically higher. An individual with a bachelor's degree is projected to earn 75 percent more over a lifetime than someone with a high school degree alone, and that figure rises to a staggering 275 percent increase in income potential for someone with a professional degree as compared to a high school graduate.[4] Meanwhile, employers are increasingly encouraging their workers, regardless of age, to seek more training or education. In a national survey, the figures are fairly consistent across age levels, with 39 percent of employees aged 50 to 64 being encouraged to improve their education and skills, as compared to 35 percent of 18- to 29-year-olds and 35 percent of 30- to 39-year-olds; even 25 percent of employees aged 65 and over were encouraged by their employers to seek additional education (see Exhibit 4–3).[5] Clearly, one's economic viability is increasingly linked to one's level of education and, for the first time, the currency of one's education. "Lifelong learning" has moved from being a catch-phrase to an absolute necessity.

This ever-increasing importance of education, and particularly higher education, is being driven by the continuing transformation of the American (and particularly the Californian) economy from an industrial/manufacturing base to an information/knowledge base. The dynamic nature of this transition cannot be overstated. The business environment continues to witness wave after wave of consolidating, downsizing, rightsizing, and refocusing on core processes. The labor market is characterized by a steady erosion of manufacturing jobs, whereas knowledge-based occupations are expected to experience large increases over the next several years.[6] This trend is exacerbated further by the explosion in telecommunications and information management technologies and the revolutionary pressures they are creating as they penetrate further and further into the nation's socioeconomic fabric. As Botkin and Davis put the case in *The Monster under the Bed*:

[4]U.S. Department of Labor, Bureau of Labor Statistics, *Occupational Outlook Quarterly*, Spring 1995.

[5]Don A. Dillman, James A. Christenson, Priscilla Salant, and Paul D. Warner, *What the Public Wants from Higher Education: Workforce Implications from a 1995 National Survey*, Social & Economic Sciences Research Center, Washington State University, November 1995.

[6]U.S. Department of Labor, Bureau of the Labor Statistics, *1996-97 Occupational Outlook Handbook*, 1996.

Exhibit 4–3
HAS AN EMPLOYER ENCOURAGED YOU TO GET MORE WORK-RELATED TRAINING OR EDUCATION IN THE LAST THREE YEARS?

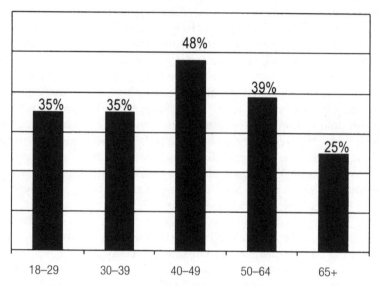

Source: Washington State University, SESRC, *What the Public Wants from Higher Education*, November 1995

The merger of computers, telecommunications, consumer electronics, publishing, and entertainment is the economic equivalent of geological plate tectonics. Industries instead of continents are bumping up against each other, and knowledge is the volcanic lava liberated from their merging and blending. We are experiencing nothing short of a revolution in learning and the knowledge business.[7]

This convergence of computer and communications technologies has sparked an explosion of knowledge generated by the analytic power and knowledge-sharing their integration makes possible:

The sum total of humankind's knowledge doubled between 1750 and 1900, and again between 1900 and 1950, and again between 1950 and 1960, and again between 1960 and 1965.

[7]Jim Botkin and Stan Davis, *The Monster under the Bed: How Business Is Mastering the Opportunity of Knowledge for Profit* (New York: Simon & Schuster, 1994), 48.

It's been estimated that the sum total of humankind's knowledge has doubled at least every 5 years since then, and that
by the year 2000 97% of what is known will have been discovered or invented [in our lifetimes]. It has been further
projected that by the year 2020, knowledge or information
will double every 73 days.[8]

Thus, as the volume of human knowledge itself continues to expand exponentially, the value of education and "learning how to learn" will
continue to rise dramatically.

The explosive growth of the Internet parallels and supports this
dynamic expansion of knowledge and information. According to MIT's
Nicholas Negroponte, the number of Internet users is doubling every
year, while user demand for bandwidth (a line or network's capacity for
carrying digital traffic) increases by a factor of 10 annually.[9] It is estimated that 2.7 trillion e-mail messages will be sent in 1997, with e-mail
volume projected to increase to 6.9 trillion messages annually in the
year 2000.[10] MCI has projected that data traffic will exceed voice traffic
on global phone systems by the end of the decade.[11] The current and
projected expansion of the Internet is largely attributable to one key feature: the making of information- and knowledge-sharing independent
of time and geography (and at a relatively negligible cost per transaction). It is this central characteristic of network technologies that offers
the potential for further increases in economic productivity and the continued transformation of the world economy.

Unfortunately, those most likely to be in leadership positions in
both the public and private sectors also are likely to be the least knowl-
edgeable about or comfortable with the network technologies that form
the Internet. Again, Negroponte notes that digital literacy (the ability to
effectively understand and engage in the digital environment of the Internet) is almost universal among American children currently in grade
school and junior high, with senior citizens having the next highest level

[8]James B. Appleberry, in comments presented at the 1997 AASCU-NASULGC
Annual Meeting, *Public Higher Education Shaping the Future, Setting the Pace,*
Washington, D.C., November 17, 1997.
[9]"The Changing Technological Environment," speech by Nicholas Negroponte,
Head, Media Lab, The Massachusetts Institute of Technology, to the 18th International Council for Distance Education World Conference, *The New Learning
Environment: A Global Perspective,* The Pennsylvania State University, June 2,
1997, University Park, Pa.
[10]Susan Morgan, "Services Rush Out Vexing E-Mail Blackouts," *Web Week,* April
28, 1997.
[11]Kevin Kelly, "New Rules for the New Economy," *Wired,* September 1997, 142.

of digital literacy. Negroponte identifies those in between, including the age groups most likely to contain America's middle and upper management in business, government, and education, as the "digitally homeless" who are encountering rapidly increasing pressure to educate themselves regarding the on-line world.[12] This drive to attain digital literacy is gaining strength, particularly in the private sector, as the transformative effects of network connectivity redefine the processes, operations, and very bases of value for entire industries, including banking, publishing, and retailing.[13] Without the imperatives of rapidly changing cost structures and sources of profitability that are pushing their private-sector counterparts, colleges and universities have been content largely to employ information technologies in their administrative functions; they have been much slower to integrate them directly into their fundamental instructional activities. However, shrinking government budgets and increasing service demands are substituting for the profit motive in forcing higher education institutions to consider seriously how advances in information technology may completely restructure the ways in which we educate and the very nature of our industry.

Because of the fundamental need for education if one is to survive and prosper in the information economy, the demands placed on educational institutions at all levels by the state and the general public are growing. In a national survey, 57 percent of respondents placed improving public education at the top of the national agenda, ahead of reducing crime, reining in the federal deficit, and reforming campaign finance laws.[14] Furthermore, a survey of state legislators from across the nation had between 80 to 90 percent of respondents ranking teacher preparation, undergraduate education, and K–12 reform as top priorities for colleges and universities; only 56 percent felt the same about graduate and professional programs, and fewer than a third of state legislators surveyed identified basic research as a priority for higher education (see Exhibit 4–4).[15] Clearly then, the nation is focused on improving public education as a means of economic survival, and expects colleges and universities to play a significant role in making that happen. It also appears that we are expected to place a greater emphasis on undergraduate instruction while

---

[12]"The Changing Technological Environment," supra n. 9.

[13]Philip B. Evans and Thomas S. Wurster, "Strategy and the New Economics of Information," *Harvard Business Review,* September-October 1997, 73–78.

[14]"American Opinion: A Quarterly Survey of Politics, Economics, and Values," *Wall Street Journal,* December 13, 1996, at R1.

[15]Sandra S. Ruppert, *The Politics of Remedy: State Legislative Views on Higher Education* (Washington, D.C.: National Education Association, National Center for Innovation and Office of Higher Education, 1996), 13.

4.2 FORCES DRIVING CHANGE

Exhibit 4–4
PERSPECTIVES FROM STATE LEGISLATURES:
PRIORITIES FOR COLLEGES AND UNIVERSITIES

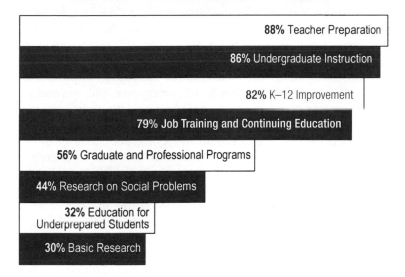

88% Teacher Preparation

86% Undergraduate Instruction

82% K–12 Improvement

79% Job Training and Continuing Education

56% Graduate and Professional Programs

44% Research on Social Problems

32% Education for Underprepared Students

30% Basic Research

Source: National Education Assocciation, *The Politics of Remedy* (1996).

working harder to convince state legislatures and the public of the importance of graduate and research programs to undergraduate education, economic development, and the overall mission of higher education.

Growing enrollment demand, declining state support, and the rising preeminence of information technology have combined to create a new set of major challenges for higher education. Never before have American colleges and universities been asked to serve so many students in such dramatically new ways, and without a significant increase in the resources necessary to undertake such efforts. The stakes have never been higher, either. Both individual and national economic competitiveness in the Information Age depend on higher education. It's just that simple, but providing that education is becoming increasingly complex. Colleges and universities particularly need help adapting to the requirements of the technology revolution. We need the resources and expertise to make our faculty, staff, and students active participants in that revolution, but we cannot look to traditional sources for the funding necessary to make that happen. Thus, these forces of change have led colleges and universities across the nation to seek new approaches and relationships that will allow them to respond effectively to the challenges of their new environment.

4.3 CHANGES IN THE STRUCTURE OF THE EDUCATION INDUSTRY

By applying the "Elements of Industry Structure" model developed by Michael Porter[16] to the current education marketplace, we can see why the changing competitive environment surrounding educational institutions, and particularly colleges and universities, necessitates the pursuit of new modes of operation, including strategic partnerships. (See Exhibit 4–5.) The industry itself includes K–12 institutions, colleges and universities, community colleges and technical/vocational schools, preschool programs, continuing education and professional certification programs, and postgraduate programs. Within this group, constant tensions over academic standards, appropriate roles and missions, competing programs, and legislatively mandated cooperation have led to rivalries over declining public resources and legislatively defined areas of operation. Higher education witnesses frequent public and legislative struggles over roles and resources between public and private institutions, liberal arts colleges and research universities, state university systems and their constituent campuses, and so on. All of these traditional, in-the-family conflicts take place within a larger environment defined by the purchasers of educational services, suppliers of educational resources, potential substitutes for existing educational activities, and possible new entrants into the higher education marketplace. Changes in these environmental factors are forcing colleges and universities to adapt through new forms of cooperation and partnership, both with their fellow institutions and with organizations outside of the higher education industry. An examination of higher education's new context may provide clues as to the ultimate direction the industry's evolution might take.

The Buyers

Traditionally, students and their parents have been viewed as higher education's primary consumers, followed by the government and business sectors. In addition, colleges and universities have found the education and certification of K–12 teachers to be one of their major markets. The development and training of higher education faculty also has been a significant internal market between research universities and other postsecondary institutions. In recent years a number of events have arisen to strengthen the bargaining power of higher education consumers, thus requiring changes by these institutions to meet the demands of the market. The rapid escalation in the cost and price struc-

---

[16]Michael E. Porter, *Competitive Advantage: Creating and Sustaining Superior Performance* (New York: Free Press, 1985), 4–10.

Exhibit 4–5
EDUCATION INDUSTRY—STRUCTURE AND DYNAMICS

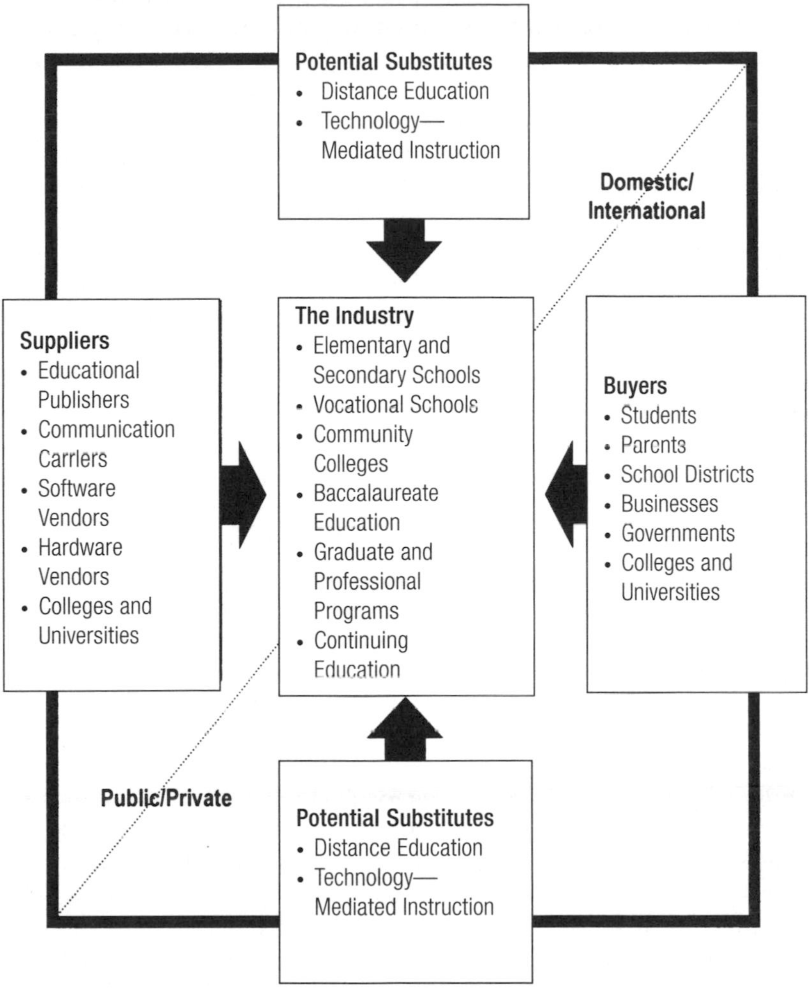

Potential Substitutes
- Distance Education
- Technology—
  Mediated Instruction

**Domestic/
International**

Suppliers
- Educational
  Publishers
- Communication
  Carriers
- Software
  Vendors
- Hardware
  Vendors
- Colleges and
  Universities

The Industry
- Elementary and
  Secondary Schools
- Vocational Schools
- Community
  Colleges
- Baccalaureate
  Education
- Graduate and
  Professional
  Programs
- Continuing
  Education

Buyers
- Students
- Parents
- School Districts
- Businesses
- Governments
- Colleges and
  Universities

Public/Private

Potential Substitutes
- Distance Education
- Technology—
  Mediated Instruction

Diagram based on "Elements of Industry Structure," from *Competitive Advantage* by Michael Porter (1985).

tures for higher education has been particularly significant. The "sticker price" for a college education has increased over the last decade and a half, often at double the overall rate of inflation. Students and their families, and the governments that subsidize higher education either directly or through financial aid, increasingly are demanding that colleges and universities contain costs by improving productivity and efficiency throughout their operations. Simultaneously, our "external" consumers are demanding greater accountability from higher education providers;

they want colleges and universities to prove that they are making every effort to use public funds and tuition dollars to produce measurable learning outcomes. For the first time, they are raising serious questions about what truly constitutes quality in higher education. They also wish to examine the degree to which our traditional definition of quality, along with its attendant institutional and faculty reward systems, effectively serves the needs of students, governments, and businesses.

Meanwhile, the dynamics of the "internal" market for higher education (i.e., the supply and demand of higher education professionals to staff the departments and programs of colleges and universities) has changed as well. As higher education institutions increasingly are affected by the information technology revolution and the swelling demand for undergraduate education, they are placing more and more emphasis in their recruitment of the future professoriate on digital literacy, the application of technology both within one's discipline and the classroom, and fundamental teaching skills. The growing recognition of their status as consumers in the higher education marketplace is likely to lead colleges and universities that emphasize undergraduate instruction to begin engaging their suppliers—research universities, and primarily the Ph.D. programs—in a conversation regarding the skills and abilities that doctoral graduates must have to be viable candidates for faculty positions. Consumer institutions have very real needs for faculty possessing teaching and technology skills, and Ph.D. programs clearly need to assist their students in finding career opportunities in what consistently has been a crowded and competitive market over the last several years. Thus, a dialogue between the producers and consumers of faculty services must be pursued with great seriousness and a full realization of its implications for the higher education enterprise.

While this questioning of traditional higher education by consumers continues to grow, employers have expanded their significance as buyers in the higher education market. As was previously discussed, the current state of the world economy has placed many companies in a highly competitive business environment characterized by continuous, dramatic change. In response, employers are asking their workers regardless of status and age to pursue further education, particularly at the collegiate level, and many are backing those requests with tuition payment programs and flexible work schedules. However, given the economic context in which they must operate, companies sponsoring their employees' educations are beginning to stress results over degrees. Regardless of the "proof of purchase" an employee receives at the end of his or her educational experience, employers want their workers to be able to demonstrate what they have learned and apply it in improving job performance.

Businesses also want to get training and education for their employees at the lowest cost to the company, in terms of both employee time and company funds. These cost and flexibility factors fuel a willingness on the part of many corporations to seek alternative continuing education providers, or perhaps to create their own in-house employee education operations. Because of the volume of students and money they may bring to the table, as well as their relatively low costs for switching education providers, companies often have significant leverage in bargaining with colleges and universities for the best deal. Although decision making about selecting a postsecondary education provider continues to be dominated by traditional notions of quality linked to resource-based reputations—concepts that have been created, maintained, and dominated by traditional higher education institutions—employers are beginning to accept, within limits, certifications and other alternatives to degrees from accredited colleges or universities for job training and career advancement purposes. Thus, for the first time, the relatively protected higher education marketplace faces the possibility of significant new entrants.

Additionally, companies that obtain training and education services for their workers from colleges and universities increasingly are demanding that specific, measurable performance provisions be included in the contracts. In these cases, if the skills or competencies that the institution's programs or courses were intended to develop are not reflected in improved employee performance according to agreed-upon standards, companies may demand additional educational services from the institution at no charge, as well as changes in course structure and/or instructor. These contracts relate institutional and faculty performance directly to student performance, and the university is held accountable for meeting student performance goals or remedying situations in which those goals are not being met.

Barbarians at the Gates, or Is That Bill Gates? (Potential New Entrants)

Imagine this scenario: You're the head of a major public university system with campuses very much in the traditional university model. You have large fixed costs in terms of plant, equipment, and tenured faculty. Your campuses operate according to the usual quarter- or semester-system calendar, with classes offered primarily during regular business hours on weekdays. Your academic programs are largely defined along fixed, departmental lines by discipline, without much crossover. Your ability to adapt your institutions to rapid change and the needs of the market is slowed significantly by complex and lengthy policy-making processes. You've just been called into the governor's office, along with your system vice-presidents and perhaps the chancellors of your largest campuses. The governor informs you that a consortium of technology firms and educational publishers has put in a bid to supply the state's undergraduate education needs below the cost of the state's current higher education appropriation. Then she asks for your bid.

Although this story is merely hypothetical (for now), how far we are from fiction becoming fact is uncertain at best. As we've noted, demands from purchasers of higher education services, including students, parents, government, and industry, for demonstrated learning and tangible (i.e., financial) results are increasing. They also are demanding at least a significant slowing in the tuition growth rate. Scheduling flexibility and programs tailored to their specific needs are becoming significant factors in their choice of service providers. Meanwhile, the barriers for entering the higher education market are diminishing, increasing its attractiveness to potential corporate competitors. Rapid advances in telecommunications and computer technologies already have opened opportunities for more flexible delivery of education within traditional colleges and universities; continuing growth in satellite and digital networks ultimately may reduce the need for physical campuses and classrooms substantially, or eliminate it altogether for some types of instruction. As technology-mediated instruction continues to develop, potential providers who previously may have decided not to enter the higher education market because of the significant capital investments and large fixed costs associated with starting a new campus may now view the return on investment ratio as tipping in their favor.

By far, the most significant barriers to entry into the collegiate market remain accreditation and government policy. Accreditation, the process of peer review and oversight by which institutions of higher education certify and maintain the quality of their educational programs, has served the important function of limiting effective participation in the postsecondary marketplace to colleges and universities able to meet certain standards, especially regarding facilities, resources, and faculty. As higher education consumers shift their focus from quality considerations based on inputs (endowments, library collections, and "star" faculty) to educational outcomes and demonstrated learning, accreditation too will have to evolve to focus more on the quality issues that concern higher education's stakeholders. In that evolution, standards and measures regarding the effectiveness of technology-mediated instruction will be developed as accredited institutions seek to expand their distance learning activities and application of technology in the classroom. Once widely accepted standards of quality for technology-mediated instruction (as defined by educational outcomes) are in place, it is less clear if accreditation will be a barrier to new higher education providers who wish to serve the market in nontraditional ways. Accreditation standards have defined the rules of the game, and as technology changes the game it is changing the rules and who may play.

There is another set of rules over and above those defined by the higher education community: those set and enforced by the federal government. Federal policy mandates certain aspects of accreditation through the certification process for participation in student financial aid programs. The recent history of unacceptable default rates and poor provision of service by certain classes of postsecondary education institutions led to federal regulations that are particularly sensitive regarding distance education. These policies restrict access to federal financial assistance for the students of schools that utilize distance education techniques as their primary form of educational delivery, and they place a significant regulatory burden on the institutions as well as the agencies that credit them. As most reputable, well-established colleges and universities seek to expand their technology-enabled operations, pressure is mounting to refocus federal policy on educational outcomes, as opposed to the method of instructional delivery, in determining access to student financial aid. At the same time, the potential of telecommunications and computer networks for maximizing higher education access (a long-standing goal of federal postsecondary education policy) is quickly being revealed, thus providing further impetus for a reevaluation of federal policy regarding technology-mediated instruction. As federal student financial aid dollars become available for pursuing higher education via network technologies, our market will become even more attractive to technologically advanced information service providers, especially when the rapidly growing market for employer-sponsored continuing education is included.

With the digital age upon us and advanced technologies becoming the basis of an emerging new economy, there will be no shortage of potential competitors. Already many large companies have developed their own corporate universities to provide for the continuous upgrading of their human capital. Meanwhile, major education publishers and technology companies, including Microsoft, are evaluating and pursuing new opportunities for serving the larger education market. Returning to our original scenario, how long will it be before they turn their eyes and efforts to higher education once the barriers of government policy and accreditation can be surmounted? As an alternative to starting from scratch, and therefore facing a steep learning curve, inevitable startup glitches, and necessary "brand" building and marketing, many companies with interest in the higher education market may look to establish relationships with existing education services providers (i.e., colleges and universities). These corporations may choose to work through joint ventures and partnerships so that they can maintain the primary focus of their business (for example, network development and technology services provision) while relying on their higher education partners to produce educational content and student services. In this fashion, traditional higher education institutions will have the opportunity to convert potential competitors into valuable allies, producing benefits for both parties and speeding the evolution of the university in the digital age. Failure to capitalize on these prospects may lead to that hypothetical governor's office scenario in the near future.

4.4 WHY CONSIDER PARTNERSHIPS?

The Partnership Advantage

In this era of rapid advances in information technology, growing demand for education services, and declining state support, institutions of higher education are increasingly searching for partners to provide the resources and expertise necessary to enhance and expand their technological capacities. Continued institutional development in these areas is critical to the delivery of high-quality teaching and learning in a globally networked environment. Leveraging existing state support and institutional resources through partnerships with other organizations could be an effective strategy for colleges and universities to achieve their strategic goals. The "Partnership Solution," as it might be called, rests on five key advantages: timeliness, currency, risk-sharing, matching competencies, and revenue opportunities. As an example, one area with powerful potential for partnering is the information technology infrastructure of universities. In this area, the "solution" might be read along the five dimensions in the following fashion:

- *Timeliness.* By establishing ongoing relationships with major hardware and software companies, the institution will be able to gain resources and expertise that allow it to alter its technology strategy and position as advances in those fields, changes in its needs, and the actions of its competitors dictate.

- *Currency.* Similarly, through the advice and support of its telecommunications and information systems partners, the institution will be able to bring its technological infrastructure up to date and then maintain its currency.

- *Risk sharing.* Rapid advances in information management and telecommunications technologies are the norm and can render major institutional investments in those areas obsolete virtually overnight. An institution can minimize its potential losses for retooling its technological infrastructure by sharing those costs with its corporate partners; in fact, this element of risk serves as a major incentive for an institution's partners to assist the university in maintaining the currency of its systems, because the costs of falling too far behind will be substantial.

- *Matching competencies.* In a partnership arrangement, both the university and its partners can capitalize on each other's organizational and operational strengths to maximize the benefits of the relationship for all parties. The technology partners can focus on supplying hardware, software, training, and support to meet the higher education institution's educational and student services needs. In return, corporate partners increasingly in need of more and better workforce training may find their higher education partners to be a valuable source of tailored educational services.

- *Revenue opportunities.* By relying on each other's strengths, both sides of the partnership equation may be able to realize significant revenue opportunities. Of course, the profit motive ultimately is the driving force behind most corporate endeavors, and partnerships with colleges and universities will not be an exception. However, the institution should recognize the potential for strategic partnerships to provide revenue streams that augment its existing base of support. Through content development projects, student and alumni services, and a variety of other endeavors, business–higher education partnerships could generate funds for the institution as well as its corporate partners, which the institution may use to maintain and enhance its academic program.

For more information on partnerships, see Appendix 4A.

4.5 PARTNERSHIP AND THE CALIFORNIA STATE UNIVERSITY

The California State University has embarked on a number of projects to take advantage of the opportunities offered by this dramatic period of change for advancing its core mission objectives of education, research, and service. Many of these efforts emphasize effective application on information management technology to meet the pressing needs of the university and the state. However, the CSU's traditional source of support, state appropriations, most likely will not be sufficient to meet its technology needs. In fact, several requests to the state to fund systemwide campus infrastructure development as a capital investment were not successful. Therefore, the CSU has sought to utilize new operational and funding structures, such as partnerships and joint ventures, in pursuing major technology projects. Perhaps the most significant example of the university's efforts in this area has been the development of its Integrated Technology Strategy (ITS), a systemwide planning framework and process for enhancing the technological capacities of its 23 campuses.

The Integrated Technology Strategy

The Integrated Technology Strategy (ITS) had its beginnings in the work of three blue-ribbon commissions led by campus presidents and composed of faculty, professional staff, and administrative officers from each campus.[17] The commissions began their work in 1993 and focused on technology issues related to:

- Instruction and academic programs
- Administrative functions and operations
- The technology infrastructure at the campus and system levels

These commissions chartered pilot projects to test ideas and provide the proof of concept necessary for structuring systemwide initiatives. Their consideration of the issues and experiences with the pilot projects led them to recognize that a formal, comprehensive, systemwide strategic planning framework and process were necessary to address campus needs for:

- Inter- and intracampus technology infrastructure
- Academic and administrative technology applications
- Financing strategies for supporting these initiatives

Thus, the ITS was born early in 1995 and designed to proceed in three phases: strategic planning, implementation planning, and project implementation and ongoing operation. The development of the ITS strategic plan utilized a number of broad information-gathering techniques, including surveys, reviews of existing documentation, and stakeholder workshops/focus groups. Assumptions, principles, and priority initiatives for the ITS were derived from these sources. With this information, the campus presidents and project staff formulated a vision for information technology within the CSU. They constructed a planning framework, which is graphically displayed as a pyramid (see Exhibit 4–6), in which the apex represents the primary strategic *outcomes* for technology identified by the CSU:

- *Personal productivity.* Empowering every student, faculty member, and staffperson to pursue their personal performance goals through access to the necessary technological tools and training.

---

[17]For further information, please see the CSU Integrated Technology Strategy website: http://its.calstate.edu/.

Exhibit 4–6
INTEGRATED TECHNOLOGY STRATEGY FRAMEWORK

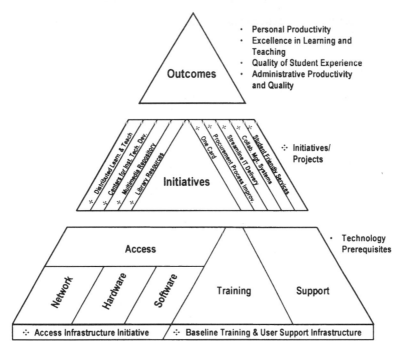

- *Excellence in teaching and learning.* Enhancing the effectiveness of learning and teaching processes through the appropriate application of an array of telecommunications, computing, and multimedia technologies.

- *Quality of the student experience.* Improving the overall quality of a student's university experience from application through graduation via technology.

- *Administrative productivity and quality.* Using information management technologies, and the economies of scale that they make possible, to increase administrative productivity and effectiveness.

A number of technology initiatives related to these strategic outcomes form the body of the ITS framework. This initial set of "first-wave" initiatives for advancing each outcome was selected from among a large number of campus and faculty proposals. Although this group of projects is by no means exhaustive, these initiatives were selected for their immediacy of need, potential impact in advancing their intended outcome, and attainability within the system's short-term constraints of budget and capacity. The initiatives include:

- *Distributed learning and teaching.* Through this initiative, the CSU seeks to use information and instructional technologies to enable faculty to meet students' diverse learning styles and needs without regard to place or time.

- *Centers for instructional technology development.* Projects pursued under the centers will focus on providing faculty with the facilities, training, and support necessary to effectively use information technology applications in their teaching.

- *Student-friendly services.* This series of efforts will lead to the development of a common electronic "front door" on the World Wide Web for colleges and universities statewide, providing a single source for students and families to access information relevant to their choice of a higher education institution.

- *Streamlining information technology delivery.* This part of the ITS emphasizes taking advantage of systemwide economies of scale to consolidate campus administrative data centers and develop purchasing cooperatives for hardware, software, and network resources across CSU campuses.

The base of the ITS pyramid is formed by the technological infrastructure needs, both campus-specific and systemwide, that must be met in order if the CSU is to accomplish its long-range strategic outcomes. The baseline technological infrastructure identified in the ITS includes not only fibers and wires but also the training and support functions necessary for faculty, students, and staff to realize the full potential of an integrated telecommunications and computing network. Through workshops and focus groups, faculty, students, and staff members impressed upon the ITS process the critical importance of end-user training regarding hardware and software applications. In essence, they taught us that human capital has to be developed alongside physical and technological capital if the university is to move forward in the Information Age. These fundamental starting points for truly integrating information technology into the life of the university—development of a baseline intracampus infrastructure and an integrated intercampus network, as well as access to essential hardware, software, training, and support throughout the CSU community—are identified within the ITS as the Telecommunications Infrastructure Initiatives (TII).

To effectively pursue the systemwide projects envisioned under the TII, the presidents of the CSU's 22 campuses (and now 23 with the addition of CSU—Channel Islands) agreed to form a Systemwide Internal Partnership (SIP) to leverage the combined size and resources of their campuses. They quickly concluded, however, that their combined strength would not be enough to achieve the TII objectives within the required timeframe (two to three years) for "catching up" to the technology revolution and meeting the enrollment demand of "Tidal Wave II." With additional state support for meeting these needs likely to be limited by budget constraints, and continuation of incremental development of campus and system technology infrastructures no longer a viable option, the CSU decided that it had to take its internal partnership external and invite information technology and telecommunications companies to join the effort.

The SIP team is not seeking gifts and donations, but rather a strategic relationship with a world-class group of technology corporations. They believe such a partnership will enable the CSU to fully develop its baseline technology infrastructure while providing attractive business opportunities for its potential corporate partners. The proposed scope of the partnership includes every aspect of the system's Technology Infrastructure Initiatives, from planning, designing, financing, building, operating, and maintaining the CSU's inter- and intracampus technology infrastructure to providing ongoing training and support for effective utilization of the technology within the university community. In return, the public/private joint venture could include the development of an education/training brokering cooperative. A possible subsidiary of this type would generate revenue through packaging, marketing, and distributing education services and products to the CSU's corporate partners, other potential private- and public-sector clients, and the individual consumer market. The partnership also could pursue profit-making opportunities through the creation of an entity to market and deliver products and services to the CSU campuses and affinity groups, as well as other organizations. By leveraging the buying power of the CSU and its industry partners, the partnership could generate savings for all concerned on their purchases of goods and services while providing profit margins from sales to external consumers. Through these strategies, it is conceivable that the partnership could become self-financing while meeting the infrastructure needs of the CSU as well as the needs of CSU's private-sector partners for an appropriate return on their investment. Negotiations between the CSU and its potential partners will determine the final nature and scope of the partnership's revenue-generating activities, but these examples illustrate some of the possibilities.

The CSU has engaged in an extensive process of inviting and evaluation proposals from teams of potential partners, rather than working with individual companies on discrete elements of the TII. The team approach was judged preferable because the SIP team concluded that the size and scope of the project would be too large and diverse for one firm alone to meet the CSU's needs. Furthermore, they envisioned a large portion of the TII's value deriving from the rapid development and seamless integration of the proposed inter- and intracampus network infrastructures and end-user equipment, training, and support. A partnership team seemed much more likely to be able to deliver a coordinated, comprehensive response to the demands of the TII than a set of individual companies with very loose incentives for working together. Therefore, the CSU requested that corporations interested in joining with the university to pursue the TII project work with each other to present team proposals.

In defining the range of companies with which to discuss the opportunities and challenges of the TII, the SIP team developed an initial pool of 88 companies that might possess a reasonable level of the resources and capabilities required for one or more major aspects of the project. These firms were then carefully evaluated through a set of criteria that included the following key requirements:

- Cultural fit with the CSU

- Shared vision of the future of higher education

- Level of executive commitment to the potential partnership

- Size and scope of presence within California

- Operational style and team stability

- Overall quality of corporate team assembled by lead partner

- Match between partner capabilities and CSU needs.

As a result of this analysis, the CSU determined that 14 companies possessed the depth and breadth of organizational/technological competencies and financial strength necessary for participation in the TII project.

The 14 firms were invited to meet with the SIP team and the CSU senior administrators for "Discovery Day," at which the potential corporate partners discussed with university officials the concept behind the TII project, the CSU's rationale for seeking private-sector partners for this effort rather than vendor/client relationships, and the initial outline for pursuing the project. Eleven companies accepted CSU's invitation, and ten firms attended: AT&T, Pacific Bell, MCI, GTE, Lucent, Ericcsson, Fujitsu, IBM, Hughes, Hewlett Packard, and Microsoft. The SIP team advised this group that, because of the range of resources and expertise required, it believed a successful partnership proposal would entail a team of technology and telecommunications firms covering the four major industries represented: communications, systems integration, communications hardware, and desktop software/multimedia. The CSU informed the potential partners that the selection process would proceed in two steps. The first phase would allow for formal conversations between the SIP team and industry partner teams and the joint development of initial business proposals. Following a review of these draft plans, a final group of two-to-four firms/teams would be selected to participate in the second phase, which would involve more detailed work with the SIP team to develop formal partnership proposals.

Six teams/companies submitted initial plans for consideration, with three teams moving on to the second phase of the selection process. Interestingly, the three second-round teams absorbed those participants eliminated in the first phase of consideration, so that all ten firms originally invited to submit draft business plans for the project were involved in the final selection process. After working with each second-round team to develop in-depth proposals for participating in the TII, the CSU selected the team that it believed offered the highest probability for negotiating a successful partnership agreement. The team, headed by GTE, included Fujitsu, Microsoft, and Hughes Global Services. It proposed the formation of the California Educational Technology Initiative (CETI) as a corporation jointly owned by the CSU and its commercial partners. CETI would be structured to develop and maintain the CSU's baseline technology infrastructure while providing other revenue-generating avenues for the partnership. Final negotiations between SIP and the GTE team were to have been completed by December 1997, with signing of the formal partnership agreement to take place in January 1998.

Finalization of the partnership agreement and TII business plan were delayed, however, until late spring or early summer of 1998 to allow for a broad level of campus and public consultation on the project. This is to ensure that the concerns of the CSU stakeholders are addressed in the ultimate structure of the partnership. In particular, the larger university community requires assurances that CETI will not encroach on academic freedom, curriculum development, educational content, or the intellectual property rights of faculty and institutions. Furthermore, the CSU must provide detailed information to its stakeholders regarding what choices students and faculty will have in end-user hardware and software, and how the selection of applications and technologies for pedagogical purposes will be made. The CSU and its potential partners already have agreed, though, that CETI will offer a wide array of hardware and software choices to the CSU community.

The CSU and its industry partners have stated clearly that all curriculum decisions and control of educational content are the purview of the CSU faculty. Both the CSU and its potential partners have agreed to honor and protect each other's intellectual property. Now the CSU and its commercial partners face the challenge of instilling confidence in the CSU's students, faculty, and staff that these commitments to the academic integrity of the CSU are an inherent feature of CETI. Through this innovative arrangement, the CSU may be able to meet its technology infrastructure needs well into the next century with no net cost to the institution for the initial buildout of that infrastructure. Thus, given the importance of technological development to the future of the CSU, the value of this public–private partnership and its potential for reshaping the largest senior system of higher education in the country cannot be overestimated.

4.6 ADDITIONAL PARTNERSHIP EXAMPLES

The California Virtual University

The California Virtual University (CVU) serves as another example of the CSU's strategy of engaging in partnerships to advance its technological reach. In the CVU, the California State University has joined with the University of California, Stanford University, the California Community Colleges, the University of Southern California, and Cal Tech to develop a common presence on the World Wide Web for marketing and distributing their educational programs and services on-line. Ultimately, any accredited California-based college or university will be able to join the CVU, with the goal being to capitalize on the state's world-class reputation in higher education to develop it as a major revenue-generating, worldwide export. The CVU itself will not be a separate, degree-granting university, however. It will build on the existing technology-mediated and distance learning activities of its constituent members to offer potential students easier access to each institution's on-line offerings.

Each student will select a "home" institution that will be responsible for providing academic advising and support services as well as granting course credit and degrees. The CSU's role will focus on linking and organizing its institutions' electronic courses and programs into a common "front door" to facilitate consumer access and choice. The CVU will market the institutions' combined Web-based catalogs to maximize their exposure in the marketplace and thus their revenue-generating possibilities. It also will seek to support the development of additional on-line courses and programs among its member institutions. In this regard, the CVU will be entrepreneurial in responding to the needs of corporate and individual clients and in developing sources of financing other than state appropriations.

With the active support of Governor Pete Wilson, the CVU has expanded from a partnership among colleges and universities to a higher education–business partnership as well. Sun Microsystems, KPMG Peat Marwick, International Thomson Publishing, Microsoft, and Pacific Bell have all joined the CVU as founding members by agreeing to contribute $75,000 each to the project. The governor intends to add to their contributions by including $14.1 million in state support for the CVU to his FY 1998–99 budget request. If approved, these funds will support:

- The conversion of courses at the CSU, University of California (UC), and California Community Colleges (CCC) to a digital, "Net-compatible" format

- The expansion of instructional technology use within the state's public colleges and universities

- The further development of the UC's Digital Library Program, which will make the holdings of the UC libraries available over the Internet

- Matching grants to financially needy students for the purchase of computer hardware, software, or Internet access

Acme Virtual Training Network

Higher education/private-sector partnerships may provide a mechanism by which colleges or universities can tailor programs to meet the specific needs of a particular company or industry. Such relationships may benefit local or regional economies through developing a well-educated, properly trained workforce for industry. They also may provide tremendous benefits to students interested in working in a particular field by ensuring that they develop the skills employers truly need. Furthermore, they enable university faculty to inform their teaching and research with the latest developments from the field, and in turn allow the faculty to share the insights from their research directly with practitioners.

One example of this type of strategic partnership from the CSU is the Acme Virtual Training Network. The CSU has partnered with Warner Brothers Feature Animation, John A. Rowland High School in Southern California, and Phillips High School in Birmingham, Alabama, to increase the opportunities for high school and college students to become animation artists. Through this nine-month pilot project, students from the high schools and San Jose State University participate in weekly two-hour classes conducted by Warner Brothers animators via a videoconferencing network supported by MCI, GTE, PacBell, Bell South, and the multipoint switching services of the CSU and the University of Alabama. Students at these sites are fully interactive with their Warner Brothers instructors in Glendale, California, as well as each other, allowing for a "virtual classroom" in which students can display their work, receive immediate critiques, and participate in real-time question-and-answer sessions with teachers or fellow students hundreds or even thousands of miles away. Students at CSU Fullerton, CSU Northridge, and Alabama's Lawson State and Jefferson

State Community Colleges also view the teaching sessions but are not interactive with the other sites.

Through the Acme Virtual Training Network, Warner Brothers is developing new sources of talent in a scarce labor market for animators, thus enabling the company to meet its needs. Meanwhile, students are receiving education in professional animation skills to which they would probably not otherwise have access and that will enable them to pursue career opportunities throughout the industry. Again, none of this would have been possible if not for the combination of complementary interests and resources brought together through a business–higher education partnership.

Distributed Learning Network for Teachers

Partnerships between higher education institutions and other entities, both for-profit and nonprofit, may enhance the ability of colleges and universities to fulfill key functions in meeting critical state needs. Besides providing access to the resources and expertise necessary to produce the required programs and services, corporate–higher education partnerships may allow a more flexible and timely response to public problems (and marketplace opportunities) than either group acting alone. This is particularly the case when advances in telecommunications and computing technology can be brought to bear on problems of educational delivery, because technological applications hold the potential for freeing the teaching and learning process from time and place restrictions. Moreover, the utilization of technology-mediated instruction may allow institutions and their corporate partners to achieve significant economies of scale in course development, especially when large numbers of students must take a relatively small number of the same courses.

In the CSU, an opportunity of this type presented itself when the state adopted a class-size reduction program in 1996 that dramatically increased the demand for elementary school teachers literally overnight. Many of California's school districts already were relying heavily on emergency permit teachers when the class-size reduction act was passed. The instant demand for elementary school teachers generated by the new state program led to an explosion in the number of emergency permit teachers in the state's classrooms. This generated tremendous demand for flexible pathways to assist those teachers in becoming fully credentialed, as they ultimately must to continue teaching. The CSU, through its business subsidiary the CSU Institute, joined with Simon & Schuster Publishing and the Los Angeles County Office of Education to build one such pathway, the Distributed Learning Network (DLN).

The Distributed Learning Network will use video, telecommunications, computing, and network technologies to enable teachers to take courses toward their credential without having to attend on-campus classes. Initially, courses will be developed for five areas of need:

1. Reading methods
2. Mainstreaming special education students in the classroom
3. Classroom management
4. Educational technology
5. Cross-cultural language and academic development (CLAD)

Simon & Schuster is financing development of 12 video modules for each course, which are being produced in collaboration with CSU faculty authors and the Los Angeles County Office of Education—Educational Television Network. Students will use the video "chapters" in conjunction with texts and coursework assigned by CSU faculty and designed to assess competency and knowledge. In addition to occasional face-to-face meetings, students will maintain contact with faculty members and fellow students via e-mail, phone conferences, and a dedicated Web page for each course. All CSU campuses will be able to offer DLN courses as an option for emergency permit teachers, and CSU campuses participating in the DLN will accept DLN courses from other CSU campuses toward a credential from their programs.

In this fashion, emergency permit teachers will be able to pursue a full teaching credential with greater scheduling flexibility, and thus they are more likely to achieve their credential in a timely fashion. Moreover, the CSU, which has historically been the major supplier of teachers in California, will be able to fulfill one of its primary missions by increasing the number of fully trained teachers in the state's classrooms. However, this would not be possible without the participation of Simon & Schuster, which in turn stands to benefit through the sale of the video modules both within California and nationally. By bringing together their distinctive competencies in partnership, the university, the corporation, the state, and ultimately teachers and their students all benefit.

4.7   CONCLUSION

As we have seen, California's colleges and universities are experiencing the leading edge of a wave of social, economic, and technological change that has begun to sweep across the American higher education landscape. Dramatic increases in projected enrollment growth, combined with declining fiscal support from state legislatures throughout the country, are putting higher education institutions between the proverbial "rock and a hard place." Add to these forces the increasing demand for public accountability, the as-yet unmeasured but assuredly growing demand for collegiate education by nontraditional students and their employers, and the unquestioned necessity of meeting the capital, institutional, and educational requirements of the high-tech revolution, and that rock begins to resemble an avalanche.

The examples from the CSU experience demonstrate that higher education institutions can do more than merely mitigate the potential damage from these tremendous environmental shifts—they may in fact enhance the achievement of their core missions, both now and in the future, by engaging in strategic partnerships. Their efforts in this regard should be predicated on a careful evaluation of potential partners according to compatibility of organizational cultures, consistency of operating philosophies, shared level of commitment to project goals, and the potential balance of resources and expertise each organization brings to the relationship. With positive findings in these areas, higher education institutions can pursue successful joint ventures that will enable them to meet their fundamental educational, research, and service missions while providing appropriate financial returns to their for-profit partners.

Given the high costs but great rewards of equipping themselves for the Information Age, colleges and universities must search for options that will allow them to expand their technological capacities within their existing fiscal constraints. However, in pursuing the partnership solution, colleges and universities must not violate fundamental tenets of the academy, such as institutional integrity and academic freedom. As the CSU discovered, carefully considered partnerships with key players in the telecommunications and computer fields can be a large part of the answer to an institution's problems in meeting its technology objectives. Together, universities and corporations can fulfill their common interests in advancing higher education while meeting their distinctive needs.

APPENDIX 4A PRINCIPLES OF PARTNERSHIP

Certain principles are helpful in developing sound partnerships between higher education institutions and other organizations (see Exhibit 4–7). The principles of partnership may be viewed in two sets: Partnership in Context and Partnership in Action.[18] The first group, Partnership in Context, includes the basic factors that must be in place for the establishment of a successful partnership. Although the Action principles provide guidelines for how the partners should relate to each other and work together to achieve their common goals, the principles

---

[18]John C. Henderson, "Plugging into Strategic Partnerships: The Critical IS Connection," *Sloan Management Review,* Spring 1990, 8–12.

of Partnership in Context mark the ground on which healthy strategic relationships can begin to develop and prosper:

- *Mutual benefits.* As noted under the advantages of partnership, there must be something in it for all parties if an equal relationship is to be built; the institution and its potential partners must see their pairing as generating strategic advantages for themselves both together and separately if their relationship is to be a true partnership and not a donor-client relationship.

- *Predisposition.* The university as well as its potential partners must possess organizational cultures and climates that will allow their working relationship to grow. Business–higher education partnerships are unique forms of public-private linkages. Corporate partners must be sensitive to the culture and mission of higher education. Similarly, colleges and universities must understand the market imperatives their possible private-sector partners face, and how the profit motive may be harnessed for the benefit of higher education without threatening its essential commitment to public service.

- *Commitment.* Finally, all parties must be dedicated to pursuing the partnership. Higher education institutions must have assurances that their potential business partners are serious about pursuing long-term strategic opportunities, not just quick profits. In return, companies that would like to form partnerships with colleges and universities require real demonstrations that the institutions have thought through and understand the full ramifications of the relationship. They need to know that the college or university will stay the course as the potentially difficult process of getting their joint ventures going unfolds.

The principles of Partnership in Context define the environmental characteristics necessary for the successful development of higher education–corporate partnerships. Thereafter, the principles of Partnership in Action identify the parameters of the partners' relationship to each other:

- *Shared knowledge.* All parties to the partnership arrangement must actively share their expertise and information pertaining to the agreement's scope. This is not to say that other areas of knowledge exchange are precluded; the parties may identify additional areas of strategic advantage in which sharing information and expertise might lead to a fruitful expansion of their relationship. However, the success of their joint ventures will most likely depend on the degree to which they establish a

Exhibit 4–7
PRINCIPLES OF PARTNERSHIP

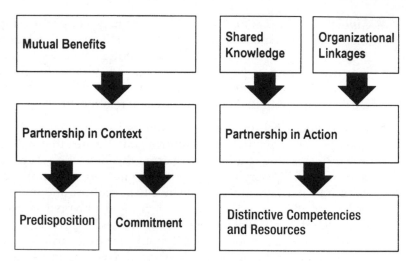

Source: John Hendersen, "Plugging into Strategic Partnerships," *Sloan Management Review,* Spring 1990.

common base of understanding regarding each other's capabilities and the problem at hand. Thus, sharing knowledge is an essential day-to-day feature of a productive partnership.

- *Organizational linkages.* Facilitating the exchange of knowledge requires solid working relationships between key members of the partners' organizations. The partners must be able to closely coordinate their joint operations; thus, relationships between the parties must begin at the executive level but then also extend down through the operational units. Besides its importance to effective coordination, building mutual contacts throughout the organizations will allow the partners to assist each other in identifying further areas where cooperation might be beneficial.

- *Distinctive competencies and resources.* Each partner must bring a unique set of capabilities and resources to the table in order for the partnership itself to make sense. The relationship should be complementary, such that the partners' various strengths balance each other's weaknesses, leaving the whole greater than the sum of its parts. By relying on what each organization does best, the partnership will enable its members to focus on mission-specific objectives and activities; essentially, each organization will be freed from having to focus resources and effort on operations that are not essential to its mission and empowered to pursue those functions for which it is most suited.

Potential Issues

By keeping in mind the dimensions and principles of partnership, colleges and universities may effectively navigate the unfamiliar waters of establishing and maintaining productive strategic relationships with private-sector companies. Higher education institutions and their potential partners also must be aware, however, of issues that can become deal-breakers in the higher education setting:

Academic ownership of content. The basic values of academic freedom and inquiry are an essential feature of the university. Thus, attempts to get higher education institutions and/or their faculty members to cede ownership of course content completely would be a nonstarter in partnership negotiations. This is especially true given that such content probably would be a major component of the value an institution brings to a higher education–business partnership. Although faculty have historically agreed to contracts with publishers that involve relinquishing rights to texts or instructional materials, such contracts are different both in size (individual faculty members in contrast to the institution as a whole) and scope (individual texts as opposed to entire course modules or programs). Additionally, their actions in this regard traditionally have been tied to meeting their responsibility for publishing original research, for which they are rewarded in the retention, promotion, and tenure process. The mechanisms for determining the distribution of benefits from joint development and marketing of courses and programs between faculty, institutions, and corporate partners have yet to be fully defined. Thus, structuring partnerships to respect and protect the intellectual property rights of all parties involved remains a central focus in establishing such partnerships.

Together, the advent of the Information Age, in which knowledge has become the primary source of economic value, and the continuing decline in state support for higher education drive the need for colleges and universities to think institutionally about managing the intellectual property created and held within their academic communities. A higher education institution would be ill-advised to enter into a partnership that involves completely relinquishing ownership of course content, both for the very chilling effect it may have on the academy and for the loss of a major source of value it may represent.

Open access to technology versus "non-compete" requirements. The diverse needs of students and faculty for technology applications appropriate to their areas of study and research require that colleges and universities support a broad range of choices for these constituents. Additionally, students' varying income levels and financial situations necessitate that institutions attempt to provide students with as many low-cost options as possible. Thus, colleges and universities most likely will not be able to accept partnership requirements that restrict student and faculty choice in hardware and software strictly to the offerings of its partner or partners.

Separating the core from the periphery.   Generally speaking, a higher education institution defines its core mission in relation to some mix of education, research, and public service. Besides these identifying functions, colleges and universities must engage in numerous administrative and support activities to sustain their essential operations. Additionally, they may have functions or operations that have developed over time which do not directly relate to their basic functions, but which are nonetheless considered an important feature of the university setting. In this era of tight resources and increasing demand, higher education institutions will seek to follow the path pursued by many private-sector companies: they will develop partnerships that allow them to accomplish support or peripheral activities while freeing resources and energies to focus on their core missions. By the same logic, universities are unlikely to engage in business relationships that compromise the reputation or integrity of their institutions by outsourcing functions central to their basic identity.

Sensitivity to academic values.   In selecting partners, colleges and universities will avoid associations with corporations that fail to exhibit sensitivity to the academy's fundamental values, such as freedom of expression, equity, and social justice. Partnerships with private-sector entities that do not respect an institution's values can damage the climate of trust and support between the institution's leadership and its faculty and students, not to mention the general public. Besides the disruptions that such relationships may generate within the university community, the potential backlash may significantly reduce the benefits of the partnership to both parties. Colleges and universities must evaluate potential partners in light of the impact the proposed relationship will have on their internal environment and their public standing; if the proposed partnership appears to contradict what the institution has defined publicly as its basic mission and values, then the relationship will be untenable.

Consideration of possible stumbling blocks such as these represents a final step that must be taken before an institution engages in a partnership of any kind, but particularly when the potential partnership includes for-profit organization in close business relationships that are relatively new in the higher education setting.

PART THREE

Taking the Expeditions to the Next Level

Chapter Five
Strategies for the Future

Strategies for the Future

JILLINDA J. KIDWELL

PricewaterhouseCoopers

GRADY MEANS

PricewaterhouseCoopers

5.1   INTRODUCTION

It is a fascinating, and challenging, time for higher education. According to some indicators, things have never been better. Industry observers, however, recognize that in spite of significant accomplishments, the industry is struggling in its attempts to deal with tough internal issues and bring about significant change. Moreover, a sense of impending change looms over the industry. Many now concur that external trends are about to force major structural change in an industry that has remained virtually unchanged for over 700 years. For the first time in centuries, the competitive environment is so intense that institutions are adopting extraordinary new strategies, for which they may be unprepared.

This chapter describes a new approach to strategy development. It is a process that injects sounder judgment about which initiatives to implement and sets realistic expectations on what results to anticipate. The process itself is subversive, as it challenges underlying assumptions about what strategy is, who is in charge of strategy, and what strategy is supposed to accomplish. It also mobilizes leaders and managers. The process readies them to engineer the strategic structure of their institution (or parts of their institution) to take full advantage of advances in technology and to pursue emerging new market opportunities rapidly.

Change is affecting all institutions. It compels all institutions to understand the forces of change and respond quickly to them. Quick and responsive institutions succeed and excel. Unresponsive institutions tend to wither. No one has a mandate for survival. It is easy to anticipate alternative approaches attracting students with technologically advanced delivery of high-quality, tailored education. It is easy to project beautiful, pristine, expensive, and slow-moving campuses being converted into golf courses and resorts if they fail to continue to be highly attractive to students at all levels.

5.2   A QUICK PERSPECTIVE

According to Richard Chait in the January issue of *Change* magazine, the achievements of higher education over the past decade have been remarkable.

> Never has the importance of a college education been more widely recognized, a realization that has generated yet another round of federal student aid, and that will fuel—along with population growth—record enrollments of over 16 million students by 2007.
>
> The economic value of a college diploma continues to climb; college graduates now earn, on average, more than half again as much as peers with only a high school diploma. Alumni contributions have soared 51 percent over the past five years. Some 270 institutions have endowments of over $65 million. Billion- and multi-billion dollar campaigns by preeminent universities, as well as comparatively ambitious efforts by largely regional colleges, have succeeded; the smart money continues to back higher education.

The proportion of 18- to 24-year-old high school graduates enrolled in college has risen from 34 to 42 percent in 10
years, from 25 to 35 percent among blacks, and from 27 to 35
percent among Hispanics. More than 415,000 foreign nation-
als flocked to study in the United States last year because the
American system of higher education has no rival. Even
among the notoriously cynical faculty, almost 76 percent of
some 34,000 respondents from 384 colleges rated "overall job
satisfaction" either satisfactory or very satisfactory in
1995–96.[1]

Against these achievements, a review of the higher education
landscape reveals that most institutions are in the midst of significant
change projects, ranging from reengineering and systems replacement
projects, to projects that select areas of academic excellence on which to
focus, to initiatives that tackle tenure issues. Many of these change projects are an outgrowth of cost reduction projects begun in the late 1980s.
At that time, reducing costs became one of the overriding concerns for
most college and university presidents. External constituents, unhappy
with rising tuition, increased costs, and inefficient operations, demanded that institutions become more cost-effective. In response to
these concerns, universities implemented a series of across-the-board
budget cuts. Although these efforts were difficult, many institutions
were able to reduce their costs through attrition, thus avoiding layoffs.
Others reduced costs through selective outsourcing agreements. Several
institutions also took on the tough assignment to reduce academic programs. They instituted strategies to invest in a selected set of programs
and to reduce their investment in "underperforming" programs.

In the mid-1990s, costs were still rising, yet the staff reduction programs of the 1980s had eliminated most of the excess administrative capacity. Furthermore, there were increased pressures to improve service
quality and increase customer satisfaction. This meant that new sets of
strategies were required to meet the demand to lower costs. Today, many
institutions are in the midst of massive efforts to replace their administrative systems and to reengineer their core processes. Though many leaders
articulate the belief that reengineering and new systems will improve
performance, provide better management information, and increase customer satisfaction, they are undertaking the difficult reengineering agenda
in part because they see the promise of reduced costs.

Where does this leave higher education today? The administrators of these institutions are stretched thin by the demands of their

[1]Richard Chait. "Illusions of a Leadership Vacuum," *Change.* 40.

existing change efforts. Significant resources are being dedicated to systems-related and reengineering projects. The capacity for change at most institutions is "maxed out." Success has not yet been declared and visions have not yet been realized. There is no established track record of success.

To exacerbate the situation, leaders in higher education traditionally have not been asked to initiate and oversee aggressive change agendas. First, they serve in an industry that has experienced remarkably little change in its core production function for centuries. Consequently, leaders are expected to preside over institutional assets, manage incremental growth, oversee institutional operations, deal with emerging ad hoc political issues, and raise external money. Ironically, at certain times in which visionary leadership has been demonstrated, the faculty rebel, making real change impossible. Faculty dissidence (actually dissonance) contributes to an environment in which some presidents are reluctant to be too radical for fear of evoking their disfavor, ultimately jeopardizing the security of the presidents' own jobs.

The absence of a strong track record in identifying and implementing change leads some to question whether higher education can develop a culture of change that it sorely needs. Can it create a culture that is ready to take on new challenges demanded by the competitive environment?

The Challenge

Whether or not higher education can develop a culture of change is a moot point. It must! New challenges are on the horizon, driven in large part by the information revolution. As industry insiders agree, the onset of the digital age is accompanied by other external trends that place higher education at the brink of massive, structural change. The current paradigm of postsecondary education (a finite, four-year experience) will be transformed into a continuum of lifelong learning exercises (K–99). Given attractive new channels for education, students will demand higher quality, learning-driven (rather than teaching-driven) options. The exchange between student and faculty member will shift to a collaborative mentoring relationship.

The very shape of the industry will change, and the rules of the game are in the midst of being rewritten. Industry lines are being redrawn to include corporate universities, nontraditional competitors, and traditional colleges and universities. Nontraditional competition is about to give higher education a run for its money. In this environment, strong participants who can readily adapt to change, define innovative strategies, and move quickly will continue to be competitive. Weak, costly, cumbersome institutions may be drummed out of business or acquired by stronger competitors. "Resort-ware" and rigid courseware may be overtaken by more efficient and better targeted alternatives.

With structural change imminent, every institution needs to consider its current position and determine what level of change it must achieve to ensure its survival over the next decade. Each institution needs to ask questions that challenge current assumptions. Where will our greatest sources of value come from in the future? Do we need to create a venture to transform the way we deliver our core programs, to capture the burgeoning market for distributed learning? What alliances do we need to develop in order to deliver new products? What do we need to do to reduce our risk in this dynamic environment? Should we merge with another institution(s) to create more value for students? What about launching offshore operations, in concert with other universities, to derive economic return on the need for educated workforces in developing countries?

These are not simple questions and they cannot be answered in a vacuum. They must be answered in the context of where the institution stands today, what it expects the future to be, and what role it wants to play in a radical new industry.

Importantly, to answer these questions, institutions have to adopt a different approach to strategy. This new approach redefines the meaning of strategy, determines the most attractive approaches for creating sustained value, and develops seamless implementation plans that address culture, processes, resources, systems, and structures.

5.3   WHAT IS STRATEGY?

Strategy is what a university does to sustain and grow its value into the future. This is a deceptively simple definition of strategy. "Does" is the key word: a strategy must be implemented quickly to be of value. Strategy is decisions and actions, not inch-thick plans, incremental budgets, and dull reports. It is not endless meetings charting general missions or hopeful aspirations. Strategy means rapidly creating and sustaining value, not just thinking about it. Strategy combines the most attractive opportunities for turning value creation into decisions and a coherent implementation process.

But how does an institution develop the right competitive strategy? Moreover, how does an institution ensure that its strategy is implemented? These tough questions do not have obvious answers. "Doing strategy" is a new phenomenon for higher education. No proven higher education methodology exists that has been tested by dozens of institutions. Rather, institutions that engage in "doing strategy" will be charting new courses. They will be adapting corporate practices and tailoring these methods for their institutions. They will be acting more like shrewd investors who need to choose a handful of solutions from among an array of potential opportunities. They will likely need to align existing structures and internal practices rapidly to support their initiatives. Because universities will be competing with effective new private-sector, for-profit institutions, they will need to begin to adopt some of the perspective and management processes of corporations. This has huge cultural implications.

Traditional strategic planning exercises evolved from financial planning and budgeting exercises to product portfolio analyses in the 1970s and 1980s (e.g., identification of strong versus weak programs as a basis for investment or benign neglect). As financial modeling became more feasible, strategy involved scenario forecasting and institutions began to predict their overall cost positions based on different scenarios. With few exceptions, the geographic boundaries that framed these analyses were the walls that defined the perimeter of the campuses. The competitive landscape included a set of peer or aspirant institutions. The student markets they targeted were relatively stable and predictable. As with any sector experiencing growth and excess demand, planning was relatively static. Except for forays into interdisciplinary programs, the programs they were marketing were largely the same ones they had been marketing for decades. Investments were incremental.

Higher education's traditional strategic planning processes may no longer apply. Nontraditional institutions may soon begin to cut into the university market in a larger way and force universities to compete more aggressively for students and revenue. Most of the strategies envisioned to date by colleges and universities are incremental and additive. Existing strategies help avoid further erosion of revenues and markets, but they are not preemptive. They may help the institution stay in the game, but they do not reinvent the game. The industry is at the brink of structural change. It needs new approaches to strategy that take into account the underlying drivers that are reshaping the industry. It needs a process to help it define transformational strategies and begin to implement them.

5.4   WHAT IS TRANSFORMATIONAL STRATEGY?

A *transformational strategy* occurs when an institution wins by changing the rules of the industry in which it competes and is rewarded by achieving a disproportionate increase in sustained value. As shown in Exhibit 5–1, strategies fall into three grades of change: incremental, substantial, and transformational. A review of the corporate world sheds some insight into the differences between the three grades of change. In well-documentedinstances, in industry after industry, market leaders

Exhibit 5–1
THREE GRADES OF CHANGE

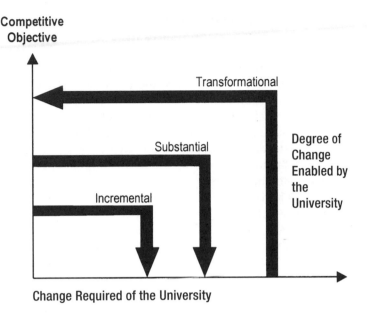

missed fundamental shifts in their industry. They missed the opportunity to develop transformational strategies. The fact that others missed the signs of impending change gave those companies that created transformational strategies the opportunity to rewrite the rules and thus capture a disproportionate increase in sustained value. Missing this shift caused established industry leaders to lose their dominant market positions. In some cases, industry members were forced to go out of business altogether.

For example, in recent years, the U.S. auto industry undertook restructuring and reengineering efforts to counter the threat of Honda, Toyota, and others. They completely missed the change in demand of the American consumer from gas-guzzlers to energy-efficient cars. They expected that the growing population of consumers would do as their parents had done, upgrading from a Ford to a Chrysler to a Cadillac. They did not foresee the need to reinvent themselves until it was too late. How does this happen? The theories abound. According to Hamel and Prahalad, in their book *Competing for the Future*, these companies did not have a strategy process that facilitated serious questions about the future. They did not consider a future that was fundamentally different from the current one. They did not develop institutional management processes to make and implement decisions to deal with market changes.

5.5   HOW SHOULD AN INSTITUTION "DO" TRANSFORMATIONAL STRATEGY?

If the operative word in strategy is *doing*, then how should a university launch a strategy process that produces the actions required to remain competitive in today's environment?

First and foremost, the strategy development process should be rapid. This differs dramatically from the traditional strategic planning process, which involves months of input from a variety of constituents and results in several volumes of initiatives. Often these initiatives are no more than a set of institutional wish lists and a budget for the upcoming year. Instead, the process should create a crisp statement of its envisioned future state and the tactics it will implement to achieve its vision. The end-to-end process should take only 10 to 20 weeks (excluding implementation). Throughout the process the leadership team should drive toward action and avoid the temptation to overanalyze during the assessment phase. Further, they should recognize that they are not developing the "perfect" strategy. Defining a perfect strategy is not possible in an uncertain environment. What counts is that they adopt the "best" strategy, knowing that it is directionally accurate. This strategy is subject to refinement during implementation.

The word *rapid* implies another set of conditions that must be in place if results are to be achieved quickly. That is, the decision-making processes to support strategy projects must be distinctly different from traditional ones. Doing strategy means that once the institution has defined its strategy, activities will be launched immediately to support the new strategy. This requires that leaders focus on a set of defined outcomes, understand what it will take to achieve them, and make decisions in a timely manner. The decision-making processes at most institutions today are either inadequate (they are cumbersome and slow) or nonexistent. To be successful, institutions must undertake an initiative to redesign, or invent, appropriate decision-making processes concurrent with the strategy development process.

Second, the process must develop the clearest picture of the future of the industry possible from today's vantage point. Articulating this picture of the future state of an industry in flux is challenging. Strategy under uncertainty adds complexity to the planning process. To overcome uncertainty and increase the chance that the future the organization describes is close to reality requires that the leadership team ask the unthinkable. They need to research existing trends. They need to understand the forces driving change in the industry. They need to form hypotheses regarding in which direction these forces will drive the industry; and finally, they need to agree on a set of assumptions about the future structure of the industry.

Third, because the future is uncertain, the strategy process should be iterative and dynamic. In keeping with the increasing rate of change in the environment, it is important that the process itself reflect the dynamic nature of the market. This means that the process should include regular opportunities to challenge existing assumptions about the future and refine the strategy to reflect new realities.

Fourth, the process must be data-driven. Strategic opportunities to create sustained value must be based on a clear, unbiased understanding of the current state of the institution: its culture, processes, resources, systems, and structure. Although "brand" intangibles are clearly important and valuable, the process must deflate assumptions about quality, status, and market position. It needs to include a cogent view of the current competitive landscape. Who is in our competitive space? How do they win against us? What are their important differentiators? What students decline our offers of admission to attend a competitor and why? What strategies do our competitors employ? What best practices and innovations exist in higher education and related industries?

Fifth, the process must become the key decision-making and management process for the leaders in the organization. Rather than being an extra, time-consuming process, it must be accepted as the main process. The institution's leaders must commit significant time to understanding the current state, delving into the drivers of the industry and determining how their university can best create a dominant position in a changing industry. Importantly, they need to develop a broad, management perspective on the opportunities for value creation. They need to understand all of the strategic and tactical issues in each functional area. Involving critical leaders in the process lays the foundation for sustaining change from the first day of the project. The strategy process itself establishes new competencies among leaders and managers in the institution. The strategy process creates a team of senior leaders. Long before implementation begins, they will have developed close working relationships, a common vision for the future, and a shared understanding of the challenges to the vision. They will be prepared to mobilize diverse resources around opportunities that may be in areas outside of each person's narrow specialty.

Finally, the strategy process must continuously focus on making decisions and on getting things done quickly. During the development of the strategy, questions must be raised and answers developed regarding the competencies and structural changes required to realize the vision. How will we get there? How do our current core capabilities transition to the future? What operations have to be realigned? What will it cost to achieve our objective? Is there an adequate return on our investment? What can we prototype to test our strategy? As the initiative moves into the implementation phase, projects must be established with approximately a 90-day implementation timeline. Longer time-lines suggest that the project may be too big and will result in the insti-tution giving up early. Shorter timelines suggest that the projects are merely sets of activities rather than strategic projects with measurable outcomes.

5.6 WHAT CORE ACTIVITIES CONSTITUTE THE STRATEGY PROCESS?

The strategy development activities described in this section form the basis for creating a schedule and a set of activities to guide institutional decision making. Taken in the order presented, they provide a high-level outline of the major activities that constitute the new approach to strategy development. Throughout the process, it will be important to keep the characteristics described in the previous section in mind. These characteristics will help the institution translate its activities into a re-sults-driven strategy process.

1. Complete Up-Front Preparation with the End in Mind

Before embarking on the strategy development process, the institution must mobilize for the effort. Proper preparation and planning are essen-tial to help ensure a successful outcome. As the institution mobilizes, it should identify the strategy leadership team, identify the objectives and timeline for the strategy initiative, articulate how decisions will be made, develop a communication plan, and determine the approach for involving appropriate constituencies.

2. Use a Solid Analytical Framework to Identify Transformational Strategies

If transformational strategies are now required in higher education, how can an institution ensure that it considers innovative possibilities? It can start by using the right framework and tools to assess the current environment (both external and internal) and by using these analyses to define future opportunities. This section describes the elements of a comprehensive assessment framework that serves three important ob-jectives: it helps create a shared understanding of the external and in-ternal environments; it organizes the results into a set of strategic issues; and it produces a set of potential strategies to overcome these issues.

Essentially, the analytical framework answers the set of strategic questions that lead the institution to describe where it is now and where it needs to be in the future to be competitive:

What is the current state of our operations and operating environment?

What is the future state of the industry? How well do our existing programs and core competencies position us to compete in this new environment?

Based on where the institution is today and where the industry is headed, what strategies are required to remain competitive? To increase market position? To rewrite the rules and create transformational change?

Out of the entire set of potential strategies, which ones are the best for the institution? Which ones can we implement?

What essential internal changes must occur to implement the strategy? What impediments must be overcome? What successful experiences can we leverage?

The analytical framework shown in Exhibit 5–2 distinguishes this strategy approach from previous strategic planning exercises. Typically, the organizing framework for strategy development relies on a SWOT analysis (strengths, weaknesses, opportunities, threats). A SWOT analysis can provide a useful starting point for a strategy process but cannot serve as the basis for developing transformational strategies. It produces ambiguous results that do not provide a clear set of conclusions. For example, many organizational strengths can also be viewed as weaknesses when reviewed from another perspective; likewise, some external opportunities can also be threats.

As shown in Exhibit 5–2, the analytical framework requires that the institution look externally at itself and the industry by reviewing markets, products, industry value chain, and the competitive environment. It also looks internally at the institution's culture, processes, people, technology, systems, and organization structure and evaluate them against industry best practices. The tools used to complete this assessment serve not only to assess the institution, but also to discover the possible strategies to overcome identified issues. An array of tools is available for use. Some are described in this chapter. Others may be found in strategy books (e.g., Michael Porter's five-forces analysis in his book *Competitive Advantage*). As it considers each tool, the institution needs to decide what information it expects the tool to provide and how much value it will add to the overall analysis.

External review. To understand the market potential, several analyses are completed. The first analysis, market segmentation, answers the question: Is there a more appropriate way to segment the market?

There are many different dimensions to market segmentation: Should it be divided by program? Geography? Industry? Customer type? Usage? Loyalty? The analysis begins by understanding the customers' contexts and developing possible segmentation schemes. Customer research with current and future customers helps determine their key concerns and the elements (quality, service, cost, time) that are most valuable.

One of the objectives of the analytical framework is to establish a data-driven, shared assessment of the current situation among the senior management team. Typically, people fail to develop consensus for action for three reasons: (1) disagreement about the facts, (2) disagreement about the future, or (3) lack of commitment to or understanding of the vision, usually due to competing and contrary objectives (a.k.a. politics). Therefore, the intent in this step is to eliminate disagreement about the facts as a basis for impeding agreement, and to establish clear assumptions about the future. This permits the institution to address the political issues from the terra firma of fact-based, rigorous analysis.

This is not, however, an exercise to "strip-mine" through data. Rather, it is an exercise based on an initial framing of possible directions and performance of selective data analyses required to test realistic hypotheses about potential issues. The institution needs to develop a set of hypotheses, derive the implications from the hypotheses, design experiments to test them, and confirm or deny the hypotheses. These hypotheses determine the scope and data requirements of the external and internal reviews.

For example, one hypothesis might be that the institution is experiencing low yield in its executive programs because it faces increased competition from nontraditional competitors that offer more flexible delivery, enhanced by technology. The implications, if this hypothesis is true, are that the institution is losing market share, experiencing higher cost per student, and losing its hold on established business relationships. Another hypothesis might be that the institution's new distributed education venture is underperforming because faculty are inadequately trained to operate in this new environment. The implications are that retention is low, refunds are high, revenues are at risk, and the institution is losing its opportunity to capture students "for life." Data are collected to test this hypothesis and confirm or refute it. If refuted, the hypotheses are reformulated and re-tested. Ultimately, statements of strategic issues, supported by data, emerge.

Customers with similar characteristics are grouped into mutually exclusive groups. A customer pareto analysis determines the relative contribution of each segment identified and is another useful input into

Exhibit 5–2
COMPREHENSIVE ANALYTICAL FRAMEWORK

Current State

	Industry	Institution
External	Market, product, industry value chain, supplier and competitor trends	Company market/product focus, value chain, suppliers
Internal	Best practices and innovations in this and similar industries	Company culture, processes, resources, systems, structure

Future State

the market segmentation exercise. The customer pareto analysis organizes customers by the amount of profit they generate for the institution. Once all of the relevant market and customer data are collected, the institution compares the new segmentation approach to the one currently in use. This comparison identifies where new strategies may make the most economic sense and what it will take to target these new markets.

As part of the market analysis, the institution will survey the political, economic, social, and technology changes that are currently driving change in the market. In light of higher education's complex, changing environment, serious attention must be given to developing a complete understanding of rapidly shifting trends. Importantly, hypotheses regarding the future must be continuously created, tested, and revised. This trend summary is the touchstone against which strategy decisions are evaluated. What are the implications of these trends? What will the industry look like in 10 years? What impact will the information revolution have on our core delivery system? What social factors are causing increased interest in educational programs?

These market analyses provide a market potential summary as input for the development of the institutional vision.

Program (or product) analysis is an important input into the understanding of the current state. In addition to evaluating programs, the analysis must identify core competencies to deliver these programs. Product profitability analysis determines the overall profitability of an institution's individual programs as well as its collective program portfolio. Program profitability analysis reviews the relative financial strength of an institution's array of products. By evaluating programs according to overall financial return, the institution can identify programs to prune from its portfolio. Conversely, it identifies where investments in programs will produce more revenue.

The pure financial return of a program, however, tells only part of the story. A three-by-three matrix (program portfolio analysis) organizes each program according to its competitive position and the attractiveness of the market. A high competitive position coupled with high market attractiveness suggests investing to grow at the maximum digestible rate. A combination of medium competitive position and medium market attractiveness suggests protecting the existing programs and concentrating investment in segments where profitability is good and risk is low. A weak competitive position and low market attractiveness suggests cutting fixed costs and avoiding investment and/or eliminating the program.

Core competency analysis elicits existing and future competencies required for launching products and services. Information is gathered on competencies that are unique and sustainable. Core competencies are typically abilities that can be utilized across program lines, markets, and processes. To be considered as core, competencies must differentiate the institution from its competitors by providing significant and demonstrable leadership. Competencies can be in many forms, including but not limited to an innovative process, a superior program, or a flexible organizational culture. These competencies are evaluated against current programs and services, planned programs and services, and competitor position. The core competency analysis is a critical step toward understanding the programs, markets, and strategies that the institution can use to compete in the present and the future. Core competencies provide the basis for developing new market entry strategies. A lack of any unique and sustainable core competency may be an indication that the institution will continue as a "follower" or should rethink its business.

The industry value chain review is designed to give understanding of the industry value chain and the institution's actual and potential niches and challenges. It describes where the institution is adding value in the industry value chain and where there is additional space in the industry value chain. For higher education, the creation of the value chain, in and of itself, is an act of discovery. The value chain now extends beyond the walls of the institution. The players include technology firms, publishing companies, and nontraditional competitors such as corporate universities. What does each player contribute to the creation of value in the market? What unique role does the institution play now? What role can it play in the future?

The final area included in the external review is the competitive environment assessment. This review answers questions such as: Who are the competitors? How are they positioned? Where are they going? There are several potential analyses that can provide insight into these questions. This review is critical for higher education today. Perhaps one of the most important tools is the competitive opportunities space analysis. As shown in Exhibit 5–3, this analysis stretches the boundaries of the current competitive space, provides a logical path for expansion into new markets and programs, and identifies which new competencies will be needed in the future. The analysis begins by identifying current programs and services that meet the needs of the existing customer base

Exhibit 5–3
COMPETITIVE OPPORTUNITY SPACE

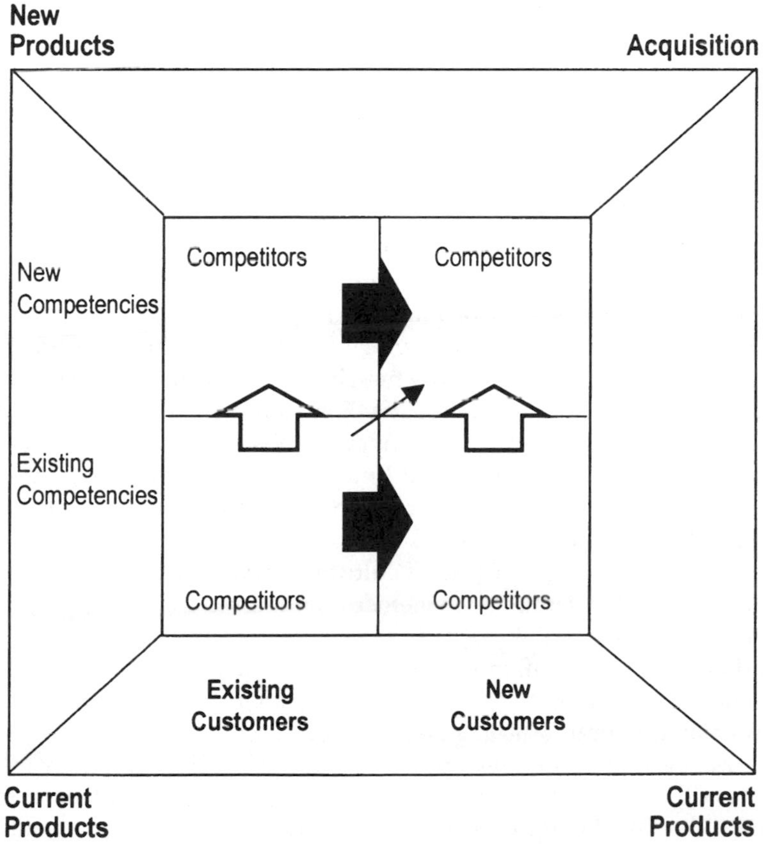

New
Products   Acquisition

	Competitors	Competitors
New Competencies		
Existing Competencies		
	Competitors	Competitors

Existing   New
Customers   Customers

Current   Current
Products   Products

and by attaching the underlying core competencies that sustain them. It then identifies new programs and services that the current customer base needs, for which the institution will have to develop new competencies. Finally, it identifies new customers that need the same underlying competencies. Once the institution identifies these opportunities, it considers the competencies of current competitors in each of the segments. The analysis concludes with the development of a strategic direction for expanding the university to serve new customers with existing competencies, existing customers with new competencies, and finally, new customers with new competencies.

Other environmental analyses can be completed. Industry alliance mapping indicates the importance of alliances in the industry and illustrates an institution's performance in creating them. A strategic positioning analysis summarizes the institution's position relative to essential competitors on fundamental dimensions.

Internal review.   The internal review should be as fact-based as the external one. As mentioned earlier, the internal review includes culture, processes, people, technology, systems, and organizational structure. Developing a clear understanding of an institution's culture is critically important, but often overlooked. What is the set of beliefs that people hold? In the end, the results an institution achieves are determined by the work activities performed by the people in the organization. These people act according to what they believe. So if an institution cares about results, it cares about how and why its people are working. Understanding those beliefs is a fundamental determinant of long-term success. Because culture is so important, it must be addressed first, not as an afterthought. The aspects of an institution's culture are conveniently summarized in a culture matrix, which lists the elements that form institutional culture on the top of the matrix. These cultural aspects include factors, beliefs, activities, and results. For example, a factor might be the perception that there is a low tolerance for mistakes. This translates into a belief that "I will be punished if I make a mistake." The activities that stem from this belief are risk-averse behavior and the result for the institution is that it suffers from a lack of radical new ideas.

Another important aspect of culture is an assessment of the current performance of essential management processes. Inadequate management processes can kill the best strategy. Therefore, it is essential to understand where the institution stands relative to best practices. The matrix in Exhibit 5–4 is a useful tool to categorize how an institution approaches decision making, communication, learning processes, and the like.

Business processes are sets of work activities. This work may or may not be adding value, but it is still work. Getting the right work done in the right order by the right people is important during implementation. Therefore, it is critical to have a robust understanding of the common

Exhibit 5–4
MANAGEMENT PROCESS ASSESSMENT

	INNOCENCE	AWARENESS	UNDER-STANDING	COMPETENCE	EXCELLENCE
Individual Commitment	None	Lip service	Team mentality	Responsibility	Group mind
Communication	No plans	Episodic	"We know what is going on."	"We understand what is going on."	"We are part of what is going on."
Team Dynamics	"How do I measure up?"	Overwhelming anxiety about people and purpose	Competitiveness; defensiveness; poor listening	Assumptions surfaced, understanding sought	Ability to frame issues and resolve them
Approach	Permission	Polite	Fun distracts	Fun supports	Creative
Conflict Management	Politics	Ambiguity	Unproductive tension and anger	Code of conduct establishes process	Challenge is encouraged and results in positive advance
Meeting Process	None	Goals, procedures, and norms unclear	Agenda	Goal, agenda, and optimum team size	Goal, agenda, optimum size leadership, and timekeeping
Learning Process	Individual knowledge is power	Communication through presentation	Knowledge transfer through discussion	Role, skill, task sharing throughout team	Interdependent Knowledge, synergistic decision making

processes that exist throughout the organization, the extent to which the organization and its activities align with those processes, and whether the processes realize maximum efficiencies. Over the past five years, higher education institutions have aggressively evaluated their core administrative processes, using tools that are now relatively common. These tools include process mapping, value added analysis, activity based costing, and work distribution charts.[2] The resources available to an institution to accomplish its strategy include people and technology. As input into the development of a strategy, several questions should be answered. What are the skill sets, technology capability, and investment currently being deployed to support existing processes? What are the skill sets, technology requirements, and investment necessary to support future processes? What gap exists between the two?

An organization has information systems and performance

[2]For a complete description of the tools and methods used to evaluate processes, see Coopers & Lybrand's, *Business Process Redesign in Higher Education* (NACUBO 1994).

measurement systems. It needs to assess the adequacy of these systems. How well do information systems meet the needs of people operating in today's environment? How well aligned are performance measurement systems with the strategies of the institution? What information will we need in the future? What key performance indicators (KPIs) are required to evaluate the strategy of the future?

Finally, the organizational structure of the institution may contain impediments to achieving future strategies. What are the layers of hierarchy? What span of control exists? How fragmented are core processes across multiple reporting relationships? A clear understanding of the existing structure, its benefits, and its issues provides insight into the changes required to be successful.

3. Determine and Categorize Potential Strategies

Once the review of the internal and external environment is complete and the drivers forcing change in the industry are understood, the institution needs to translate its findings into potential actions. It needs to make sense of the many findings.

The internal and external analyses will produce a laundry list of opportunities to improve performance and increase the institution's competitive position. As shown in Exhibit 5–5 and described in this section, these opportunities fall into four categories: (1) enterprise alignment, (2) best practice performance, (3) market/program repositioning, and (4) industry transformation. To answer the question, "What does it all mean?" the institution will summarize all of the potential strategies from prior analyses. It then will categorize them into the four groups outlined in Exhibit 5–5. Finally, it will determine the approximate economic value of each strategy.

The first category, enterprise alignment, is appropriate by itself only for institutions that have not kept internal operations current with market realities. For the most part, this strategy accomplishes incremental change. It aligns operations, but does not imply a shift in strategy. It assumes status quo in the market.

The second type of strategy includes becoming a high-performance organization, that is, achieving excellence that goes beyond best practice performance. This strategy requires a substantial level of change. The well-documented failure of many of Total Quality Management (TQM) and best practices review (BPR) efforts testifies to the difficulty of implementing this type of strategy.

Repositioning an institution's market/program focus, the third type of strategy, requires substantial change. In fact, repositioning is what most people mean when they say "strategy." The classic two-by two-matrix in Exhibit 5–6 illustrates four repositioning options. Three of the options keep either markets or programs or both relatively constant.

Exhibit 5–5
FOUR OPPORTUNITY CATEGORIES

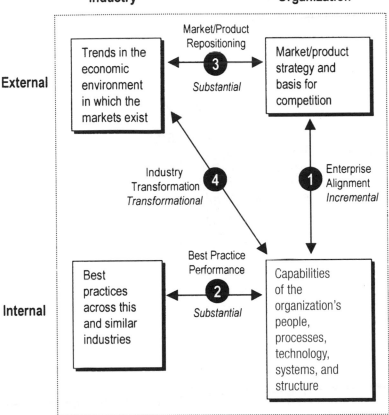

They are not mutually exclusive, although most institutions focus on getting one right. The fourth option, creating a new product for a new market, implies a new business. In the corporate sector, experience has shown that trying to do this organically has a low probability of success. Acquisitions fare somewhat better, although the burden of proof is heavy. Success is defined as synergic strategic fit and strong economic payback. Given that the acquired markets and products are new to the company, the strategic fit is often tenuous, and the economic projections vary widely on shaky assumptions.

Repositioning as a strategy will also drive operations alignment. Indeed, when repositioning strategies fail, it is more often an execution error in implementation than a factual, analytical, or conceptual error in strategy development.

Exhibit 5–6
PRODUCT/MARKET REPOSITIONING OPPORTUNITY MATRIX

	Current Products	**New Products**
New Markets	Build market reach along geographic, demographic, needs-based, or other segment dimension	Create new venture; can best be accomplished quickly by acquisition
Current Markets	Reposition current products with current customers through product differentiation, pricing, distribution and promotion	Expand product categories sold to current customers, using brand extensions, bundling, channel strength, etc.

The fourth type of strategy is transformational. The other three strategies assume that competitive conditions in the industry are more or less fixed. The alignment, high-performance, and repositioning strategies involve understanding and responding well to these fixed conditions (to the point of being able to anticipate them). A transformational strategy combines the other three and adds a dose of entrepreneurial zeal with the intent of changing the rules, and hence the competitive conditions of the industry. Transformational strategies are often resource-based, in that the institution builds a core competence that transcends current industry practice and thus creates new and attractive market/product opportunities. Corporate examples include Toyota (the lean production system); Frito-Lay (end-to-end supply chain management and the use of advanced technology); and Intel (high-velocity product development). In each of these examples, the company developed resources with a clear vision and intent for their economic exploitation on behalf of shareholders.

4. Use a Visioning Conference to Develop a Compelling Vision and Narrow the Set of Strategic Alternatives

Visioning is the bridge between analysis and implementation. A strategy should be articulated as a very precise and coherent vision of what the institution must do to sustain and grow itself. A strategic vision statement is a thorough description of the future state of the institution. It paints a picture in words and key indicators of what the institution will be at a certain point in the future. It includes a measurable summary financial target which, when attained, assures strategic success by generating sufficient economic value for the institution. The vision statement fundamentally describes what it will take to win. The following outline can be used for incremental, substantial, or transformational strategies. It should be short and include:

Economic objectives:

- Time frame
- Financial goals

Competitive positioning:

- Markets (customer segmentation and targeting; market share targets)
- Programs/services (especially portfolio life cycle management and profit targets)
- Industry value chain (supplier strategy; institutional domain; distribution/delivery strategy)

Internal capabilities:

- Culture
- Core processes
- People, capital, technology
- Systems
- Organizational structure

How does an institution develop a sound vision statement? Moreover, how does it explore strategic alternatives and commit to follow the one with the greatest economic value? Creating a vision from a white sheet of paper is typically frustrating and often deteriorates into unproductive word-smithing sessions. Before bringing the leadership team together for a visioning conference, it is critical to develop a statement of the "as is" vision. In some institutions, this vision is not on a piece of paper, nor does everyone share the same vision. Therefore, it may be advisable to list the various visions that exist in the organization. Next, the institution must create one or two alternative "straw-man" visions, based on the analyses completed earlier. At the visioning conference, these sample visions serve as a starting point to elicit reaction and to engage others in amending the vision.

The visioning conference is a three-day off-site meeting in which the leadership team and key decision makers have frank discussions about the future of the institution. The conference makes extensive use of all the data developed during the external and internal reviews. It begins with a presentation of the external analysis, followed by breakout groups in which cross-functional teams develop critical success factors. What market segments should we target and why? What factors are most critical for success in these markets? Each group presents a synopsis of its discussion. A facilitator identifies and documents consistent themes. Next, the internal analysis is presented, followed by a breakout session to determine core competencies required for the future. Again, a facilitator documents common themes. These full sessions and breakout groups can take an entire day.

The second day begins with breakout groups to brainstorm one or two overarching strategies. What must we do to be successful in the future? The group condenses these statements into a single paragraph of not more than five complete sentences and shares the results with the whole group. In the afternoon, breakout groups develop "route maps." What are the steps, methods, and activities that will achieve these strategies? What initiatives do we need to complete to see results? The day concludes with a full session in which the previously prepared straw-man visions are presented and modified.

On the third day, the group reviews the amended vision statement and then assembles into breakout groups to brainstorm impediments and to identify resources and plans to overcome them. What organizational realignment is required to be successful? Once the groups share these impediments, breakout groups convene for a final session. They develop a set of priorities for the future and share these priorities with the group as a whole. A facilitator organizes a full discussion to develop consensus regarding the most important priorities.

5. Commit to a Handful of Strategies

Decisions at a visioning conference are necessarily provisional. Like shrewd investors, leaders must base their strategy decisions on robust business plans. These business plans state the linkage of the project to the institution, develop project controls, and communicate clearly the project's strategic and financial objectives. They include assumptions, uncertainties, and sensitivities that will best indicate what the fiscal impact of the changes will mean to the institution. To provide a more complete evaluation, business plans provide the means of measuring and comparing each project's effects and benefits. (See Exhibit 5–7.)

Exhibit 5–7
OUTLINE FOR A BUSINESS PLAN

Market Segments
- Who/Where will the program target?
  - Geographic area
  - Demographic profile of student
- What are the characlerisitlcs of the target market? Why will people want to participate in the program?
  - Interesting hobby?
  - Requirement for continuing professional education or certification?
  - Worker retraining?
- What is the size of the potential market?

Programs
- What will the program offer?
- How will this program capitalize on existing strengths? What core competencies are required?
  - Leverage existing faculty skills and expertise? Access ncw resources?
  - Build on acknowledged areas of strengths? Acquire new ones?
  - Use existing infrastructure? Create new capabilities?
- What measures will be uscd to quantify success?

Financial
- What investments will be required to develop the program?
  - Course development
  - Marketing
  - Space
  - Technology
- What are the costs of ongoing operations?
- What prices will be charged?
  - Tuition
  - Financial aid/scholarship
- How much revenue wlll be generated? In the first year? In subsequent years?
  - When will the program break even? Make a profit?
  - What assumptions are included in the financial model?

Risk
- What is the nature of the competitive landscape?
- How does this tie to our existing initiatives?
- Are there new market entrants?
- Who are the competitors?
- How sensitive are the financial assumptions?
- Can the program still generate viable revenues if those assumptions are wrong by 10%? 25%? 50%?

Importantly, they include measures that will monitor the initiative to determine whether the program achieves its envisioned results.

Once the senior leaders reach consensus on the best strategy, they need to ratify their decisions and include the appropriate decision makers in the decision-making process. The structure of the strategy process was designed initially to be the decision-making process. As such, the ratification of the strategy should be relatively straightforward and a natural outgrowth of the governance structure for the strategy development project. Depending on the ramifications of the proposed strategies, however, additional steps may be required. Board approval may be necessary. Faculty approval, if not included in the overall process, is essential.

6. Communicate Extensively

Once the strategy is approved at all levels, institutional leaders begin a deliberate process to gain commitment throughout the organization. A carefully crafted communication program should commence immediately. As part of that communication strategy, the institution can organize a series of meetings to discuss the business plans. These meetings accomplish four objectives. They serve as a sounding board for the new projects, obtain important feedback, help socialize the transformation process, and garner broad-based support.

Senior leaders must promote intensive communication of the vision to all others who influence performance across the institution. This communication builds understanding, develops consensus, and encourages commitment. The vision was developed by those who are key implementation players at all levels of the institution. Now they are prepared to develop operating targets and action plans at the unit level.

7. Create an Integrated Set of Implementation Plans

Specifying a winning strategic vision is not trivial; implementing it is truly difficult. Both must be thought through at the same time. Successful strategy implementation starts on day one, with the selection of the strategy team. The team should include key decision makers, implementers, and those with significant influence over strategic direction.

Before it begins implementation, the institution needs to integrate the new initiatives into a program plan (linking the new initiatives and ongoing initiatives). The program plan includes a portfolio of projects sequenced in order of priority. The program plan also includes a description of the governance structure required to provide adequate oversight, define project charters, and assign roles and responsibilities.

During the planning process, people came together in cross-functional project teams to specify what the institution must do day-by-day to succeed with the new strategy. Now, during implementation, they are positioned to implement these plans using operating measures and targets to manage per the strategy they helped to create. In successful implementations, these front-line plans are integrated into an economic model of the strategy and a business plan that outlines the investments and payoffs expected from the strategy.

5.7 IN SHORT

Higher education is in a state of flux. The competitive landscape is intensifying. Traditional strategic planning processes that produce incremental, rather than substantial or transformational, change are no longer relevant. Instead, higher education must adopt new strategy processes, guided by a comprehensive analytical framework. As shown in Exhibit 5–8, external and internal reviews of the institution and the higher education industry generate a robust set of strategies that will change the organization and potentially change the industry.

Exhibit 5–8
TRANSFORMATIONAL STRATEGY

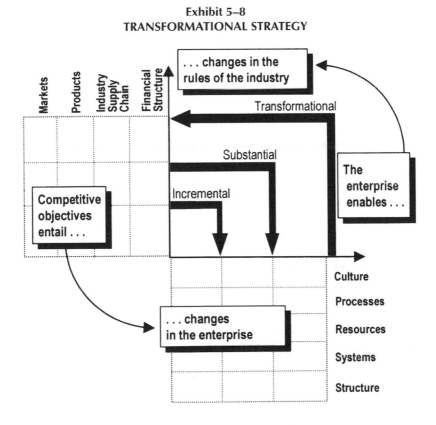

Index

INDEX